PURPOSEFUL WEALTH MANAGEMENT

UNTIL YOU KNOW YOUR PURPOSE,
HOW CAN YOU MAKE PURPOSEFUL DECISIONS?

BY
TOM WARBURTON

ACKNOWLEDGEMENTS

The author would like to thank John McCormack, Brian Bailey CLU ChFC CFP CASL, David Carpenter JD, Michael Harker PhD, Steve Holloway CIC, Phil Lakin CFRE, Mark Morley CFP, Mary Ann Norfleet PhD, and Gary Richter CPA for their generous and invaluable technical assistance.

THIS BOOK IS DEDICATED TO
ALL WHO MADE IT POSSIBLE:

My clients, who seek to build great lives for themselves, their families, and their communities.

My mentors, who continue to teach me
what "good" looks like.

My advisors, who keep me safe and on course.

My wife, the lovely Miss Vicki,
who makes me a better person.

Our family, which makes it all worthwhile.

CONTENTS

FOREWORD

If you are a person who wants to simplify your life and live free of financial stress, with time to devote to the activities, relationships, and interests that form your own personal definition of a meaningful life, this book is directed to you.

As a psychologist interested in the meaning of money to individuals and families, I have seen poor wealth management lead to huge (and sometimes enduring) problems in people's lives. There is a large body of literature in the field of behavioral economics that describes why people make irrational decisions about money and how people tend to make poor decisions about financial risk management. Whereas unwise choices can lead to restricted financial resources over time, wise choices can positively influence a lifetime of investing that can result in big dividends over time. Ultimately, long-term financial goals can be achieved, and this can lead to retirement years free of anxiety about having "enough" financial resources to live "wealthy to 100."

Managing wealth for individuals and families is a field that has advanced from the days when brokers simply managed their client's portfolio of stocks and bonds without regard to the client's lifestyle, goals, or values. The old days of money management have evolved to where the best financial managers now view their role as comprehensive wealth managers—personal chief financial officers for their clients. They are like symphony conductors who may call on collaborative participation from specialists in many different areas, in order to develop a synchronized plan specifically tailored to each individual or family client. Today's wealth managers may enlist the help of accountants, estate attorneys, insurance agents, and other specialists to ensure that their clients have tax-efficient and comprehensive wealth management focused on meeting the client's goals.

Purposeful wealth management is a key to formulating and implementing plans that enable the growth of our financial resources over time, in a manner that frees us to pursue happiness in whatever ways we choose. Purposeful wealth management creates a customized financial plan that addresses your lifestyle priorities and long-term and short-term goals—all within the framework of values that give coherence and meaning to your personalized objectives.

Most people want to maintain the lifestyle from their peak earning years throughout their lifespan. They want to be financially independent throughout their entire lives—and they often want to leave a financial legacy to family members and/or favorite charitable interests. A comprehensive wealth management plan addresses these concerns and establishes a systematic path for implementing and achieving these aspirations.

This book can help you only when you start applying its principles. Sometimes we're like the grasshopper, and sometimes we're like the ant. We want to enjoy things now, like the grasshopper, or we wisely implement methodical plans to prepare for the future, like the ant.

Purposeful, comprehensive wealth planning and management will release you to focus on the projects and enterprises that are most meaningful to you. It can improve your quality of life by leaving you time for the people you cherish and the activities you enjoy. Tom Warburton gives a blueprint for that process in this book. His ideas will encourage you to organize your thoughts, clarify your goals, prioritize your needs, and develop your own personal wealth management plan. Read this book, apply its principles, and give yourself the gift of time to pursue your personal vision of happiness.

Mary Ann Norfleet, PhD, ABPP
Adjunct Clinical Professor
Department of Psychiatry and Behavioral Sciences
Stanford University School of Medicine

Senior Research Fellow
Mental Research Institute
Palo Alto, CA 94301
www.mri.org

July, 2012

INTRODUCTION

Our mission at Warburton Wealth Management is simple: We help our clients make work optional and maintain that status.

We believe every investor is benefited by ascertaining if their goals, values, needs, resources, and obligations are realistic by reviewing the current status of their wealth management.

Sometimes things look fine—that's terrific! Sometimes things need work.

If you want to make work optional—and maintain that status—this book might be useful to you.

Life has been good to me, and now, for me, work is optional. My financial affairs are arranged such that, absent economic disaster, my wife and I are, as I like to say, "Wealthy to 100" and we will be able to maintain that status. Further, there will be money left over for our children, grandchildren, and for our Warburton Family Foundation.

So why do I work?

The answer is easy: Because I love it.

I love interacting with people who are fun, smart, and interesting. I love helping clients clarify their life goals, understand their financial options, and coordinate the moving parts of their financial lives. Helping people use their wealth to accomplish what's important to them brings me joy.

This is probably not something your friendly neighborhood stockbroker, insurance salesperson, banker, or attorney does daily. He or she may be charming and may offer excellent service, but few of them attempt or aspire to coordinate all the moving parts of their client's financial life.

I have seen wealth happen many times. I've met people who have won the lottery. I've worked with people who inherited wealth, who have grown a company and sold it for millions, who own land that sits atop newly proven oil and gas (or coal or water) reserves. There are surprisingly many people who have been magically transformed, generally as a result of their risk taking and hard work, from treading water to having millions.

Just because you are fortunate enough to reside in this seat in the stadium—having wealth—does that mean you're prepared for the responsibilities?

Just because you're wealthy, have you been trained to manage wealth? Skills are developed through lots of practice, learning, and experience over time. Managing wealth is a skill, like becoming a world-class athlete or a successful business owner.

Now that you are on the path to making work optional, will you take advantage of the tools and opportunities used by well-informed wealthy families?

Life can get in the way. Day-to-day obligations may be distracting. Is it obvious where to turn? Are you aware of the many tools and opportunities that exist?

With this book, I hope to heighten your awareness. If your goals, values, needs, resources, and obligations are in balance and you want to make work optional, this book is for you.

This book is also for you if, like many Americans, you have a sneaking suspicion that your retirement savings are inadequate. You might be concerned that work is never going to be optional.

Whatever your station in life, the investment and wealth management principles outlined herein will apply.

CAREER ODYSSEY

I've been an entrepreneur all of my life.

I started my first personal service business when I was eight years old and several others before I graduated from college.

After college, I worked in a business founded by my father in Coffeyville, Kansas. We had three employees and four customers. Our gross revenues were about $200,000 annually. We had clients in Oklahoma and Kansas.

I welded, drove the forklift, became a machinist, kept the books and, generally, did everything necessary to run a small business. Once I had a grip on the production, administrative, personnel, and finance elements of our enterprise, I hit the road as a salesman.

Over the next twenty years our company grew to become one of the largest industrial valve sales and service companies in the central states and the Rockies.

As our success grew, I began to live large. At one point, my monthly lifestyle burn rate (the amount of money I spent to maintain my standard of living) was well in excess of the annual earnings of most households.

Then I had a realization. I no longer wanted to be a slave to hotel rooms and airports. I wanted a sustainable rhythm for my life. So I sold everything. At age forty-seven, I was the president of nothing. I enthusiastically decided I would never work again.

I did what I thought any red-blooded American would do—I went to the golf course. I played over eight hundred rounds of golf in three years. But something unexpected happened. I discovered that this newfound life of leisure wasn't very satisfying. Heck, it wasn't satisfying at all!

Then one day, like a bolt from the blue, as I was standing on the practice tee mindlessly launching golf balls toward the horizon, I had a vision. I saw my grave. My lifelong best friend stood over me, saying, "There goes Tom. He came into this world with a lot of energy and quite a few skills, and he just hacked it around the golf course the last half of his life."

I resolved that "hacking it around the golf course" would not be my legacy.

I knew I needed something to do. During this "golfing phase," I happened to be the client of private banking groups in some prominent financial institutions. Their work had always fascinated me. Now, I discovered a new purpose: that of being employed by those same private banking groups that had been of service to me.

DISILLUSIONED WITH TRADITIONAL WEALTH MANAGEMENT

So, I went back to work.

After nineteen months in the trust department of a prominent super-regional bank, I was recruited by a globally prominent firm ("GPF") to help manage the wealth of high net worth individuals. Incidentally, when I worked at the super-regional bank in the trust department, our target client was a widow or orphan with one-half to two million dollars to invest. Then, when I worked for the globally prominent financial services firm, our target client was liquid for $25 million or more. (If you had $20 million, they referred to you as "almost wealthy.")

I did well with both of these firms. But eventually I faced an ethical dilemma. It turned out that no well-informed person could believe in the products they wanted me to sell.

Objective academic data proved to me that the GPF was selling "clever shiny things," but not offering the financial instruments that would enable investors to most efficiently achieve their goals.

I took a long, deep look at the historical evidence and concluded that it is impossible to beat the market. (I'm convinced that over the long haul, no one can beat the market, "time" the market or consistently pick "winning" stocks.) But the GPF that employed me was asking me to "sell" their ability to beat the market.

As I studied the discipline, these experts made the most sense:

- Eugene Fama, widely recognized as the father of modern finance and the Robert R. McCormick Distinguished Service Professor of Finance at the University of Chicago;

- Kenneth French, co-creator of the Fama/French Three-Factor Model and the Roth Family Distinguished Professor of Finance at Dartmouth College;

- Harry Markowitz, widely recognized as the father of modern portfolio theory, a Nobel Laureate and Adjunct Professor of Finance at the University of California in San Diego;

- And legions of other academicians espousing the virtues of financial science.

I'll have much more to say about what financial science tells us about investing later in the book. For now, I want you to know what I believe.

1. Unless you have access to the best passively managed funds in the world, you should invest in broad-based index funds. (Index funds are superior to active management but inferior to the products offered by Dimensional Fund Advisors. More on that later.)

2. You should own the market and abandon efforts to beat the market. Never, ever buy a single stock, no matter what you've heard.

That's a very quick summary of the investment piece of this book. But there is something else I learned at the globally prominent financial services firm and the super-regional bank: wealth management has many moving parts, and unless those parts are coordinated, the entire plan may collapse in rubble.

That means looking at investments, taxes, estate planning, insurance, charitable intent—everything. That's the comprehensive coordination I believe is critical.

This is a book created for all investors. The goal of this book is to offer a wake-up call that says, "If you've got wealth now or plan to have it in the future, these are the factors you need to address."

While I cannot direct every reader to an appropriate wealth management firm in his or her area, I can give advice regarding the questions you should ask, the questions a wealth manager should ask you, and the qualities to look for in a wealth manager. I hope you find that this book is interesting and useful, that it conveys the above referenced information, and that it helps you achieve your financial goals.

—Tom Warburton

A Bowl Full of Life
(Putting It All in Perspective)

The bowl sat in the temple all but unnoticed. It was made of fired black clay shot through with starbursts of minerals, and its glazed surface was rough. It measured two hand spans from rim to rim.

"Let us fill this bowl," the Master said. He began to add brown stones the size of hen's eggs, worn smooth by centuries in the river. "Is the bowl full?" he asked when he could fit no more stones within it.

"Yes," the Disciple replied. The Master smiled.

The Master then produced a box of pebbles, most the size of green peas, and he poured them into the bowl. The pebble peas flowed naturally to fill the gaps between the river rocks. "Is the bowl full?" the Master asked again.

"Er...yes," the Disciple said, uncertain of where this lesson was going.

Next the Master withdrew from his robes a leather pouch filled with sand. He poured the sand into the bowl, and it flowed into the gaps between the river rocks and the pea pebbles. "What about now? Is the bowl full?" he asked.

"Yes, it is full," the Disciple replied, "I think." The Master subtly smiled.

Finally, the Master produced a pot of tea and proceeded to pour its contents into the bowl. The fragrant liquid completely filled all remaining spaces. "Now," the Master declared, "the bowl is full."

The Master paused to give the Disciple time to process what he had demonstrated. Then he said: "The bowl represents your life. The large river jack stones represent the truly important things: God, family, children, health, friends, and passions. These are the things that, if every other thing were lost, would remain as the foundation of a full life.

"The pea pebbles are the things that matter, like your job, your house, and your car. But while they matter, they can all be replaced, even though you may have to work long and hard at it.

"The sand is everything else—the small stuff. A parking ticket. A tree falling down in the back yard. Your heater or air conditioner going on the fritz. Countless other everyday annoyances."

"That makes much sense, Master," said the Disciple. "But I do not understand how it relates to daily life."

"Ah," the Master said, "but it does. If you put sand in the bowl first, there will be no room for the river rocks or the pea pebbles. Your bowl of life will overflow with the small things, leaving you nothing for what's really important.

"As for the tea that topped off the bowl, no matter how full your life may seem, realize that there is always room to share some tea, or some wine, or just some time, with a friend.

"This is what makes a full and satisfying life."

(The original concept for the above story is courtesy of an anonymous source.)

CHAPTER I

PURPOSEFUL WEALTH MANAGEMENT

"What do you value about money?"

This is the first question I ask in our initial meeting with a prospective client. Without fail this simple question has an impact. Some people quip, "I know I'd like to have more of it." Others say they've never thought about it.

The second of nearly seventy questions covering everything from professional goals to personal relationships to individual interests is similar but more focused: "What in particular do you value about money?"

Among the responses are terms like "freedom," "fun," and "security." Some people will even advise that money means status. You might be surprised how competitive some wealthy people can be and how nonchalant others can be—even when they have more money than they could possibly spend in a lifetime.

Or, as I like to say, they have enough money to be wealthy to 100.

My firm views our initial meeting with prospective clients as "the discovery interview."

The goal of this meeting is to clarify the client's *purpose* (their goals, values, needs, resources, and obligations). Both the client and our company need to know what the individual hopes to accomplish with his or her money (a topic we'll explore in more detail in the next chapter) and why the client embraces his or her unique beliefs.

After all, if we don't understand the goals, values, needs resources, and obligations of our client, how could we ever hope to provide purposeful advice?

Let's examine the overall concept and various processes involved in purposeful wealth management.

THE PURPOSEFUL WEALTH MANAGEMENT APPROACH

Purposeful wealth management is based on knowing the client's goals, values, needs, resources, and obligations.

All advice and all decisions are made with the uniqueness of each individual's purpose in mind.

Unlike traditional money management, purposeful wealth management encompasses and coordinates all the moving parts of a client's wealth.

What's the opposite of "purposeful"? I'd say, "the pursuit of incremental unnecessary wealth by attempting to identify shiny things" or "return chasing."

A "shiny thing" holds the promise of above-market returns—and it's clever. Oh my gosh, it's clever!

It might be a fund that has a $500,000 minimum. It's exclusive. It's fun to talk about at cocktail parties. You can hear people saying, "Wait till I tell my friends about this deal!"

Or it might be a hedge fund. Hedge funds are shiny things because they promise that they're going to deliver equity-like returns with bond-like low volatility. Who wouldn't want that? It's the best of both worlds.

However, I don't believe that can be done consistently over a statistically significant period of time, as we'll see later.

Consultation

Once your goals, values, needs, resources, and obligations are more clearly quantified and qualified than perhaps they have ever been in your life, the next step is to develop a plan to manage the moving parts of wealth management to achieve everything that is important to you.

The best way to do this is, in my opinion, through a consultative process that addresses the relevant components of wealth management.

A disciplined and comprehensive process addresses the following:

1. Goal clarification
2. Investment management
3. Advanced planning
   a. Wealth enhancement (taxes)
   b. Wealth transfer (estate planning)
   c. Wealth protection (insurance)
   d. Wealth sharing (charitable giving)
4. Relationship management

Purposeful wealth management demands a coordinated and integrated approach. Indeed, coordination is the key. As I've said, it covers all the moving parts of your financial situation and demands that the moving parts work together.

Let's think about this for a moment. How can your tax advisor or CPA help you achieve your goals if he or she doesn't interface closely with your investment manager?

What about your estate planning attorney? How can this advisor help you achieve your goals if he or she doesn't thoroughly understand the assets and liabilities of your balance sheet along with your desires for charitable giving?

Unfortunately, this is the reality in many instances. Most investors have their insurance with one company, their investments with another, and their estate planning done by a jack-of-all-trades, friend-of-the-family attorney—and none of these folks ever talk to one another!

How in the world can anyone expect to achieve, let alone identify, his or her goals when the right hand doesn't know what the left hand is doing?

In spite of the intellectual capital resident in the firms I worked for, I never saw the consultative, comprehensive, or integrated wealth management approach practiced or applied.

THE FAMILY-OFFICE EXPERIENCE

All wealth is relative, of course. But it is true that the ultra-wealthy behave differently than the merely high net worth family. Among those behaviors may be setting up a "family office." One very prominent family office is "Room 5600"—the Rockefeller family office. This "family office" occupies the 55th and 56th floors of 30 Rockefeller Plaza in New York City. It coordinates and manages every aspect of the family wealth, which has been estimated to be as high as $110 billion.

For those with less wealth, there is the multi-family office, provided as a business model by numerous firms to provide similar, but less personalized, services.

Regardless of size, focus, or number of families they serve, you can be sure of one thing: family offices take a coordinated approach to every aspect of wealth management.

If you are not among the ultra-high net worth families, you are not shut out of the benefits of having a family office. You can instead turn to a firm that practices consultative wealth management and delivers the family-office experience.

The key is to find a wealth manager who can help you identify your goals, values, needs, resources, and obligations, and then help you achieve everything that's important to you by enlisting and coordinating a network of trusted advisors possessing important and focused services.

THE CONSULTANT NETWORK

As a personal chief financial officer for our clients, I not only make a special effort to help clients clarify their purpose, I also focus on learning everything there is to know about their wealth management needs. Everything!

Sometimes their situation is a complete mess. Sometimes it has so many bandages on it that you'd think it had been in a car wreck. Sometimes it looks like confetti thrown into the air at a wedding. Sometimes the individual has everything neatly buttoned up but isn't happy with the people he or she has been using—and the lack of coordination among those various specialists.

I have regular in-person meetings with clients. The frequency of these meetings is driven by their desire, the status of their wealth management, and their immediate needs.

I often tell clients, "You're the CEO. I'm your personal CFO. I will do whatever you want, but I will also give you independent, unemotional, disciplined, and objective advice." I do my best to match each client with the CPA, estate planning attorney, institutional-class insurance specialist, or other specialist who is best suited for that individual. We don't sell, we advise, and there are never any referral fees involved.

The great advantage to the client of me serving as a personal CFO is that when I take our client to interview a CPA, attorney, or insurance professional for consideration, I can quickly communicate the client's goals, values, needs, resources, and obligations. I also know the status of the client's other wealth management planning. Finally, I have done the due diligence and know the core competencies, quality, and trustworthiness of the professional advisor to whom I'm introducing my client.

THE IMPORTANCE OF COMMUNICATION

Speaking of CPAs, here's a good example of how purposeful investment and consultative wealth management can work.

Most people don't talk to their CPA more than once a year, and that's only when they walk in with a shoebox full of receipts and cancelled checks and plop it down on the desk at tax time. They don't realize that there's an opportunity here—an opportunity to enhance their wealth by optimizing their cash flow through tax minimization.

Our company seeks to identify CPAs who are consultative and who bring ideas to the table, as opposed to CPAs who only provide the perfunctory service of filing annual tax returns.

For example, we have an older couple as clients. We ran their numbers and determined they were going to need an extra $40,000 in a particular year. We analyzed their balance sheet of bonds for immediate currency and stocks for future currency, and we discovered a complex asset allocation, an asset location issue, and a cash requirement puzzle.

So we called their CPA and said, "We want to know what this couple's earned income is going to be this year and what their tax bracket is. We want to know if we should take this $40,000 out of one of their IRAs because they haven't earned much this year, or, if they have earned a lot and are in a higher bracket, should we take it out of their taxable account?"

The CPA said, "I'm about to fall out of my chair. You're the first financial advisor who has ever called me to ask for my advice on a situation like this in advance. Mostly I see this stuff after the train has left the station and it's too late to do anything about it."

The problem is that most clients don't call their CPA because they don't know what to ask. We do. That's the kind of service that firms like ours provide. It's not just so-called "clever investments."

We'll cover each of these topics in more detail later in the book. Right now, let's take a look at that often overlooked element: relationship management. It can mean many things, but one of the most important is making sure that once a client's wealth management is in place, it stays in place.

RELATIONSHIP MANAGEMENT

A client might call me and say, "Tom, I've got this great opportunity to invest in this new restaurant with my son-in-law, who has never been in the restaurant business but seems to be a smart kid."

I might say to him (diplomatically, of course), "Correct me if I'm wrong, but you've always told me you primarily value security. If you invest $100,000 in this new restaurant and it works, does it genuinely move your needle in the direction of security? And if it doesn't work, is it likely to be such a setback that you're risking what's most important to you?"

I also have a client in the oil and gas business who is forty-five and has a net worth of $8 million. I asked him what he wanted regarding his financial planning. "I want to be secure," he said. "Of course, I also don't want to start over again."

"Is there anything more important to you than that value?" I asked.

"Money's a score card," he said. "I've got a bunch of buddies who have $20 million, while I only have $8 million. I need to get to twenty because my buddies have twenty."

My sister, psychologist Dr. Mary Ann Norfleet, an expert in human behavior, has often reminded me, "People compare themselves to their friends. They tend to be satisfied about their wealth only when they feel they are as wealthy as their friends." How crazy is that?

My client's goals (security and a scorecard) were in complete opposition. So I said to him, "Look, as it stands, you're wealthy to 100. Your wife's wealthy to 100. You've told me what you want to do for your children and your parents and the world at large. We've got this nailed to the wall. You have won the wealth accumulation game. Are you willing to risk all or a portion of what you have to try to get to $20 million? Are you willing to risk what you already have in pursuit of incremental unnecessary wealth? If you are, we might want to consider taking your $8 million and putting it on the nose of a fast-running horse or discussing other, better considered risks in pursuit of incremental unnecessary wealth."

This is a client I often have to rein in. He comes in, and he's got wild ideas. He's inclined to pursue immediate gratification and chase performance, whether it is stocks, bonds, or private deals. I do enjoy listening to him. He's fascinating and always has his ear to the ground for a great story.

Ultimately I'll say something like, "You've got some interesting deal flow here. Let me run this past my buddies. They're experts in this field. Let's get their independent, objective advice and meet again in a week. Between now and then, I want you to remember that you told me your primary goal was 'not having to start over.' You've got it nailed. You've got security. To what extent would we risk this security in pursuit of the shiny thing?"

He would come back in a week, and I would present our analysis. We'd discuss the issues.

My preface speech would eventually come out. "You're the CEO, and I'm your personal CFO. Here's the risk. Here's the potential reward. Here's my recommendation. What do you want to do?" After all, it is his money!

So...what does the client decide to do? Well, it depends. I've had clients decide to make risky investments and I've had clients decide to not make risky investments. The element of the outcome that pleases me, whichever way it goes, is that any and all subsequent decisions are made with both eyes wide open to risk and return.

Purposeful wealth management involves all of the elements we've discussed here, and more. The key point is this: Regardless of your current or potential future wealth, everything rests on a foundation of clearly defined goals.

That's what we'll turn to next.

CHAPTER 2

CLARIFYING YOUR PURPOSE

This is the chapter you may be inclined to skip. You may be tempted to race ahead to get all of my secret investment tips and advice (the kind you read about in *Money, Kiplinger's, Smart Money,* and the other publications in the financial press that proffer the financial hype that stimulates our emotions with "noise").

Please don't do that.

The most important step in purposeful wealth management is assessing your goals, values, needs, resources, and obligations.

Until you make this assessment, how can you hope to make a good decision? Until you make this assessment, you can't know what your purpose is.

This is the most important chapter in the book.

As I mentioned earlier, whenever a prospective client comes to us, the first thing we do is schedule a "discovery interview." It can last up to two hours, and the first question is always, "What do you value about money?"

Often, when I ask that question, the person's eyeballs roll up, they look toward a far corner of the room, and they say, "Man, that's a good question. I never thought about that before. I can't believe I haven't considered that before."

I've had many folks cry when I take them through this exercise. Perhaps it's because it's so fundamental. It gets down to why you are on this planet. What do you hope to achieve? What are you trying to achieve?

Are the decisions you've been making consistent with your goals? Do you have a clear idea what those goals are?

This is a process in which investment generalists don't engage.

Before I saw the light, I was trained to ask a perfunctory ten to twelve questions about a client's wealth and risk tolerance and then immediately try to sell him or her something.

That's not how I believe it should be done or how our firm does it. We know that everything builds on this "discovery meeting"—a collaborative and consultative client self-assessment.

Only after you've figured out your goals can you invest purposefully to increase your likelihood of achieving them.

MONEY, HAPPINESS, YOUR PURPOSES AND GOALS

We've all heard the phrase, "Money can't buy happiness."

That may not be exactly true. Money can definitely buy a certain kind of happiness.

Released in mid-2010, a Gallup survey, which they hailed as the "first representative sample of planet Earth," was designed to examine the relationship between income and well-being for about 96% of the world's population.

What made the poll distinctive, in addition to its scope (136,000 people in 132 countries), was that it distinguished between overall life satisfaction and positive day-to-day feelings.

It turns out that overall life satisfaction has a great deal to do with your income or wealth compared to your neighbors.

Commenting in the *Washington Post* (July 1, 2010, page A02), Daniel Kahneman, professor emeritus of psychology and public affairs at Princeton, said, "When people evaluate their life, they compare themselves to a standard of what a successful life is. It turns out that standard tends to be universal. People in Togo and Denmark have the same idea of what a good life is, and a lot of that has to do with money and material prosperity."

Day-to-day feelings, in contrast, have more to do with enjoying life, smiling, laughing, sadness, depression, anger, feeling respected, having family or friends you can count on, and how free you are to choose your daily activities.

"What we didn't know before," Professor Kahneman said, "is the extent to which life evaluation and emotional well-being are so distinct. When you look at the books about well-being, you see one word: happiness. People do not distinguish."

Discovering what makes you happy, whether it's "happily pursuing your professional goals" or "happily pursuing your personal goals," is the first step in purposeful wealth management.

THE DISCOVERY INTERVIEW

Exchanging information is the central thesis of the discovery interview. It is anything but rigid, but one way or another, we cover the following major areas:

- Values
- Goals
- Relationships
- Assets/Liabilities
- Advisors
- Process
- Interests

As you would imagine, the questions under "Assets/Liabilities" and "Advisors" are designed to get an overall picture of your wealth and of the professionals with whom you've been working. Ultimately, we want our clients to understand why they are working with their current set of advisors.

Far more important to the process of goal clarification are values, goals, relationships, process, and interests. Below, we consider each of these and try to communicate a flavor of what's involved.

VALUES

What do you value about money? What in particular is important to you about that value? Is there anything more important than that value?

As I've mentioned, that first question usually brings people up short. They've never thought about their money that way. When folks have thought about their money, it's been in a vacuum, from the myopic perspective of "more is better" rather than "how much do I need and why."

Answers to the follow-up questions could be, "Money is a way of keeping score, and I like feeling like a winner." Or, "I have always wanted to feel safe and secure." Or, "It's a good thing. Everybody knows that."

Answers to the third question, about whether there is anything more important, vary, of course, but often they concern having good health and good interpersonal and family relationships.

GOALS

Now we get more personal. What are your top accomplishments? What would you like them to be?

Answers to these questions provide insight into what has driven a person in the past and what drives him or her today.

What would you like to do for your children, parents, other family members, or close friends?

Is there something you want to do for the world at large?

Answers to questions like these provide insight on core values, as well as contingent financial liabilities that may need to be considered.

Do you feel satiated regarding houses, boats, planes, cars, and jewelry?

In dollar figures, how much money do you need or want?

Some folks have everything they want, and some folks want lots of incremental stuff.

This informs us regarding decisions about providing future currency and establishing targets for liquid net worth accumulation.

Very few of us ever sit down and think about all of our goals. We may say, "You know, honey, I'd really like to spend two weeks in Tuscany."

Rarely do we meet folks who have looked at their goals comprehensively, to facilitate decisions that need to be made purposefully. (There is that word again—purposefully!)

RELATIONSHIPS

With the topic of relationships, the interview becomes even more personal.

We ask about important family relationships (spouse, children, siblings, parents, etc.). We also ask about relationships with people at work, people in the community, and whether clients consider themselves introverts or extroverts.

Responses to these questions provide lifestyle insight. For example, introverts don't seem to need as much money, while highly social extroverts exhibit higher levels of lifestyle burn rate.

PROCESS AND INTERESTS

The "process" questions give a clearer idea of how involved you want to be in managing your finances and how you prefer to work with your wealth manager.

I'm convinced that there are only two types of people in this world: those who are determined do-it-yourselfers and those who appreciate the value of working collaboratively with expert advisors.

My company is loath to enter into relationships with folks who don't want or value advice. Neither we nor they should enter into a relationship that is destined for divorce.

The "interests" questions deal with sports, TV and movies, books, hobbies, social time, travel, charitable work, etc. In short, how do you like to spend your leisure/discretionary time? What would an ideal weekend/vacation be like?

I've observed a lot of correlation between age and interests. Youngsters often place no premium on relaxing, and they fill every moment with activities— which usually translates into "expense." Older folks often place a high value on down time.

In fact, for older clients, I can't count the times that I've heard how puttering around the house constitutes an ideal weekend, and, similarly, "Travel is just a big hassle."

I suppose you can classify the preceding questions as "getting to know you purposefully."

Once we know our clients—and help them know themselves—we are in a position to provide advice that responds to the unique nature of each individual.

NEXT STEPS: WEALTH MANAGEMENT PLAN ASSESSMENT MEETING AND BEYOND

After the discovery interview, we schedule a wealth management plan assessment meeting as the next step in our process.

At this meeting, we review the uniquely personal information that we have gathered from our prospective client and present it within this framework: "Based on your goals, values, needs, resources, and obligations, is your portfolio purposeful, is your tax management optimal, is your estate planning current, is your risk management comprehensive, and are your charitable intents being funded?"

We look for the strengths of and gaps in current planning. We know that we won't get everything right based on our initial meeting, but we can hit all the high points and establish a baseline for work that needs to be done and projects that need to be put in our "parking lot."

At the conclusion of the wealth management plan assessment meeting, we've usually done a good job of exploring whether or not it makes sense for us to work together.

We know our process isn't right for everybody. Not all investors are appropriate for us. Our style of service is not for everyone. Unlike the typical retail stockbroker, a purposeful wealth manager doesn't want as many clients as he or she can get. We are interested in working with clients who are fun, smart, goal-oriented, and coachable. We serve a select group of clients mutually compatible with us for whom we can add a lot of value and to whom we can deliver a superb family-office experience. The majority of our clients are business owners, professionals, executives, or retirees.

If we've concluded that we can add significant value and we would enjoy working with the prospective client, we ask him or her a very straightforward question. "Would you like us to help you?"

If it's agreed that we would have a mutually beneficial relationship and our company would be able to add significant value, we schedule a mutual commitment meeting. Actually, I should say, a "not so fast there, pardner" meeting.

Assuming we do decide to work together, we ask our new client to come back a week later. We continue to reflect on how the first two meetings felt. If we elect to work together, we start opening new accounts and planning to manage the client's money according to the plan that we mutually derive.

Following the mutual commitment meeting is a 45-day meeting when we assist our new client in understanding and organizing the paperwork that our independent third-party custodian will have mailed to them. We discuss what to throw away, what to keep, and why.

Following that, we engage in a series of regular progress meetings. In these meetings, we start executing on advanced planning action items and ticking off the projects in the parking lot.

As our clients' personal chief financial officer, it's our job to look for gaps, compile action items for consideration, and propose thoroughly considered solutions in a consultative and collaborative manner.

Of course, the longer we work with a client the more we learn and new initiatives emerge. Needs are dynamic, and they change as our clients personal and professional lives change.

Prioritizing action items is a critical exercise. Elephants must be eaten one bite at a time. By meeting with our clients at regular progress meetings, we get things done. It may take quite a bit of time, but all aspects of wealth management will be buttoned up incrementally—and in a manner that is consistent with our client's goals, values, needs, resources, and obligations.

HOW MUCH IS ENOUGH?

This is an important issue.

Having enough and knowing that you have enough are two different issues. There are practical elements and emotional elements involved.

The biggest determinants of calculating enough are: what is your age; what is your lifestyle burn rate; what is your mailbox income (the money that arrives periodically from all sources, including social security, pension, dividends, bonds, etc.); and are you okay with spending your last dollar on your deathbed.

Like the old story about the squirrel that stored up acorns for the winter, we are accumulating our own acorns during our working years—we amass savings, retirement funds, and other sources of income to draw on during our retirement years.

The longer you need to financially support your lifestyle or annuitize the "acorns" you have accumulated, the more acorns you need.

The magnitude of your mailbox income minimizes the need to annuitize your acorns.

An interest in leaving a financial legacy to your beneficiaries may require more acorns.

As a general rule, a sixty-five-year-old married couple with no debt, no children in their home, spending $10,000 per month, with $4,000 per month in Social Security income and content to spend their last dollar on their deathbed will need a minimum of $1.5 million. I describe this scenario as semi-fragile. It requires very careful planning.

Increase their liquid net worth to $2 million, and the scenario moves closer to bullet proof.

Increase their liquid net worth to $3 million, and they will have the luxury of showing off with conspicuous consumption, leaving money to their heirs, or making charitable bequests.

Although all wealth managers make exceptions, the time and energy required providing the breadth and depth of services mandated by the family-office experience imposes a practical minimum client size of $1.5 million or more. Of course, having that amount of money today is not mandatory, provided the client is goal-oriented and willing to commit to a plan such that accumulation of that amount is realistic.

Before I sign off with this chapter I will say it one more time: clarifying your purpose is a necessary first step and the foundation of purposeful wealth management.

CHAPTER 3

EVERYTHING YOU'VE BEEN TOLD ABOUT INVESTING IS WRONG (PROBABLY)

There is a world of difference between *wealth* management and *investment* management.

Wealth management is the superset that encompasses everything: taxes, insurance, estate planning, charitable giving, and investments.

Investment management is just one part of this larger picture.

Unfortunately, for many people, regardless of their level of wealth, investment management boils down to a stockbroker calling up and saying, "Our best idea for you right now is…"

That's no way to invest. Among other things, you have no idea whether the proposed investment holds promise—or whether the stockbroker's manager came through that morning offering higher commissions on that particular security or on moving the firm's inventory of bonds.

I've met many people who demonstrate this behavior.

They want someone smart who says, "I have figured out this little known stochastic moving average convergent/divergent interfaced with volume aberrations, and I can spot market inflection points. I can predict in advance when the market's going to quit going up so we can sell and go short. Then I can predict when the market has met the bottom and is going to start moving back up."

It's mesmerizing! It's seductive!

Who in the world doesn't want this? It's the Holy Grail.

The problem is: It does not exist. It is an unobtainable "shiny" thing.

The plain truth is that no one—no institution, no investment manager, no phalanx of computers—has consistently demonstrated an ability to beat the market.

The next chapter presents the hard data—decades of it, in fact.

In this chapter, I'm going to ask you to go with me and, temporarily at least, accept the fact that no one can consistently earn more than market returns—especially over a statistically significant period of time.

If we're talking about wealth, we are certainly talking about "a statistically significant period of time"—the long run.

THE UNHOLY ALLIANCE

Who pays the salaries for all the columnists you read in *Money, SmartMoney, Kiplinger's,* and the like, or the onscreen talent you see on CNBC, and FoxBusiness? The answer: banks, mutual fund companies, brokerages, and other firms that want you to spend a lot of money on stock trading commissions.

Do you know where these firms get the money to make these media buys? From the people paying the trading commissions!

Things make even more sense when you pull back and take a look at the information these outlets are providing. I could give you hundreds of articles and TV segment titles, but I don't have to. All you have to do is watch CNBC for half an hour while the markets are open and score the number of segments that can be interpreted as smart people trying to persuade you to buy or sell a given security. (I particularly enjoy the conflicting buy/sell opinions spewing from the mouths of the smart people.)

Gold futures are up. Winter wheat is down. China is going for a hammerlock on rare earth metals. Google plans to introduce this new gizmo that has the potential to revolutionize whatever. What's the smart play?

RIPPED FROM TODAY'S (AND TOMORROW'S AND TOMORROW'S) HEADLINES

Like many sitting judges, I am incapable of defining pornography. Wikipedia defines it as "the explicit portrayal of sexual subject matter for the purposes of sexual arousal and erotic satisfaction." But I believe pornography is not limited to sex. I believe there are other varieties of pornography and they all have certain things in common—they stimulate our emotions and, perhaps, move us to action.

In particular here I am thinking of what I observe as "investment pornography." Permit me to define investment pornography as "the portrayal of investment opportunities for the purposes of arousing interest and stimulating trading."

Investment pornography appeals to our basic instincts (greed and fear) at a level where we cannot stop reading, watching, or fixating.

Investment pornography is grounded in fantasy. You can invest in the next blockbuster stock at the very beginning; you can buy this house for an incredibly low price, remodel it, and flip it for a huge profit; or you can invest in these properties or securities and become rich. Fantasy!

On a recent stroll through Barnes & Noble, I picked up a copy of a major publisher's magazine. I was appalled.

The cover featured a stack of $100 bills. The main headline: "Ten Ways to Make Real Money Again." This was surrounded by the following other eight article callouts:

- Stop worrying about a double dip
- Five awesome values in stocks
- Two great ways to invest for income
- Three real estate bargains not to miss
- Quiz: Do you have what it takes to be rich?
- Keys to a perfect credit score
- Save 30% on your next vacation
- How health reform can help you now

Another magazine was no better.

The cover art was focused on the right back pocket of someone wearing blue jeans, with said pocket overflowing with $20, $50, and $100 bills. Headlines:

- Our annual rankings: This year's winning funds
- Ten great funds that pay big dividends and high interest
- Put more cash in your pocket
- How sex drives your investing
- The best reward cards for you
- Cars that cut your fuel bill
- Follow our twelve new financial rules of thumb

What in the world is going on here?

These were two financial magazines published by two highly respected companies, and they both looked like nothing so much as financial versions of *Manifest Your Dreams*.

Suffice it to say that investment pornography is out there, in the mainstream, and many people with money fall prey to it.

This is precisely what the publishers of those magazines and the companies that buy advertising in them intend.

Don't be seduced. Get some objective, fee-based, fiduciary advice, and then decide in a consultative manner what purposeful actions you need to take. There is no rush. Do it right!

Ladies and gentlemen, paying attention to investment pornography is madness. If you are willing to be objective, if you are willing to let go of your cherished beliefs, you will realize that the vast majority of the information that is churned out by print, the Web, TV, and other outlets is based on a fundamentally flawed premise—that given the right information at the right time, you, too, can achieve returns that beat the market. That premise is the shiny thing.

This is unlikely to be achieved over a statistically significant period of time. But there is so much money to be made promulgating this myth that you can expect it to continue as long as there are myopic and uninformed investors to buy into the concept—and there is no shortage of this type of investor.

I'll go even further. In my opinion, in traditional money management, investors are merely hiring managers to speculate for them in the capital markets. They hire managers to rub dead chickens on your money. It's like voodoo.

Traditional financial management is misguided.

One of my friends has an acquaintance who left the brokerage business to become a teacher. He didn't want to focus on selling the products dictated by his big-name brokerage firm. He felt the firm was primarily interested in high volume buying and selling of stocks and bonds ("churning" accounts) and in selling things that promoted the firm's self-interest over their clients' best interests.

Strong words, I agree.

Consider this: Investment managers and stockbrokers don't make any money unless you buy or sell something—they have a primal incentive to encourage you to do so. The vast majority of the investment services industry has an incentive to make you believe you can beat the market with their advice.

Every year the *Wall Street Journal* publishes a list of the most successful fund managers in the business. From one year to the next, a few of the same names may appear, but rarely in their previously ranked spot. There will always be names that did not appear on the previous list—and names that will not appear on subsequent lists.

In other words, there is no A-Team of fund managers who year-after-year beat the market.

The advertised celebrity investors are intelligent, well-educated men and women at the most prominent firms who possess inordinate amounts of stock and market information. Their desire is for you, Mr. and Mrs. John Q. America, with five million dollars, liquid, to believe that you're going to consistently earn above-market returns if you hire them.

I humbly suggest that you think again.

Do you really believe that the majority of men and women of wealth actively trade stocks?

I can tell you that they don't. Instead, they develop a plan with a consultative wealth manager and let it work over time. Wealthy families do not receive a "retail class" experience, with their stockbrokers calling frequently to suggest they buy or sell some investment. They receive an "institutional class" experience, with their investments being managed purposefully toward the achievement of their goals.

This could mean that their advisor would work with them to figure out what they need to spend each year and then put enough money to cover fifteen years of that "lifestyle burn rate" into short-term, investment-grade bonds. The rest would then go into long-term investments where it can be left to "capture the expected returns of the capital markets" over the next fifteen-plus years. Having made this commitment to discipline, they do not worry about the day-to-day ups and downs of the stock market.

BONDS FOR CURRENCY, STOCKS FOR GROWTH

The way to insulate yourself emotionally and practically against inevitable market ups and downs is to have fifteen to twenty years' worth of living expenses in short-term, investment-grade bonds.

This will give you the emotional and practical flexibility to live your life the way you want while the market plays itself out.

My rule: hold bonds for immediate currency and hold stocks for long-term growth, with those stocks being converted into bonds when market opportunities permit.

The financial cable channels are tremendous proliferators of investment pornography. The information they provide on why you should buy a given stock is completely worthless. It is designed to get people excited so they will trade more. Or to buy "commission rich products" like buffered return-enhanced notes, derivatives, or other clever products. The information is not designed to help investors—the information is designed to generate revenue for the firm by selling product.

If you need a specific example, all you've got to do is turn on CNBC. Somebody with a Harvard MBA will be on there, and he or she will be the chief investment officer for J.P. Morgan. Another somebody with a Stanford MBA will be on, and he or she is the chief investment officer for Goldman Sachs. They both have access to a wealth of data and meritorious research teams. Then, for some bizarre reason, they will each have diametrically opposed positions on, say, Microsoft.

One will say it's time to buy. The other will say it's time to sell.

The only thing a well-informed investor can conclude is that they are both speculating. They are guessing!

Almost every red-blooded American is walking around looking for something good to invest in. The fact exists that—in a vacuum—there is no such thing. There's a purposeful way to invest your assets, but absent planning based on uniquely personal goals, values, needs, resources, and obligations, there's no way to know whether any investment will be good or bad in advance.

Informed investors know they succeed by enlisting the coordinated talents of niche experts. Uninformed investors believe they're supposed to be like Bob Vila in *This Old House* and do it all themselves.

Just look at the whole E*TRADE thing. Wall Street wants you to believe that you can do it yourself, and "it's only eight bucks a trade." Do you think Warren Buffet or Bill Gates is sitting around trading on E*TRADE?

No. The worst thing you can ever do is pin your hopes on any individual stock. You should never do that. Concentrated positions are two-edged swords, and you have no better than a fifty-fifty chance of lining your pocket rather than cutting your throat.

Nor do the majority of wise wealthy people take risks to accumulate unnecessary incremental wealth.

If you're wealthy to 100, and if you've got the right insurance and estate plans in place, it doesn't make good sense to take the risks you'd have to take to add (if you're lucky) yet more money to your sufficient nest egg by speculating.

Informed, sufficiently wealthy people become interested in three things: maintaining their lifestyle, achieving their goals, and minimizing their risks.

Wise wealth managers realize this and do their best to guide clients in that direction.

Now, I have to digress for a moment. Purposeful wealth management is not all "cold showers and root canals," a phrase I first heard from the liberal columnist and commentator Mark Shields on PBS's *The News Hour*.

Investing can be fun, like blackjack or poker or any other game that allows you to bring some skill to bear. (Games of pure chance hold no interest for me.)

I do make occasional non-index fund investments. It's called being "part of the club."

Every now and then some of my "good ole boy" friends and I sit down after a round of golf and discuss our real estate, or oil and gas, or other investments. We might even pull out our pool cues and roll a few balls. It's fun to talk about investments.

But I have two rules. First, I will never make any investment that might threaten the wealthy-to-100 structure I've constructed for my wife and myself. Second, I never invest more than 1% of my investible assets in any one deal. I'm happy to have my toes in a lot of ponds. But I never want to be up to my neck in anything.

I am not willing to shoulder the real risks that are attendant with the unbridled pursuit of unnecessary incremental wealth.

THE INVESTMENT ANSWER
BY DANIEL GOLDIE AND GORDON MURRAY

In 2010, Daniel Goldie and Gordon Murray published *The Investment Answer.*

Both co-authors had a great deal of experience with Wall Street. Unfortunately, Gordon Murray also had a great deal of experience with brain cancer. He knew he was going to die. Before he did so, he wanted to tell the world about his insights into successful investing.

A former bond salesperson for Goldman Sachs, he rose to managing director at Lehman Brothers and Credit Suisse First Boston before retiring in 2001. He then turned his personal portfolio over to Dimensional Fund Advisors, a company founded by academics and dedicated to financial science.

"I learned more through Dan [Goldie] and Dimensional in a year than I did in twenty-five years on Wall Street," Mr. Murray said.

Dear reader, if you have read this far, I strongly recommend that you read Goldie and Murray's eighty-five-page book, in particular, "Chapter 4—The Active versus Passive Decision."

I'll close this chapter with a reiteration: everything you've been told about investing is wrong—probably. My advice is that you turn off the "noise" from the financial talking heads and embrace financial science.

CHAPTER 4

SMART INVESTMENT DECISIONS

When I was employed by the globally prominent firm (GPF), I was always in charge of raising a crowd for presentations by stock pickers, market timers, and purveyors of clever shiny things.

We would bring some genius in from California to give a speech. I'd be in charge of getting people to attend this presentation so they might become our clients.

Each of these speakers would always have some clever scheme. Oh, they'd made 48% last year, 20% annually for the last ten years and—blah, blah, blah— here's how they did it.

Most of the people I'd attracted to fill the audience would be impressed with the dazzling intellect of the speakers. Giving credit to the attendees, I suspect they would be skeptical as to whether the performance was sustainable; however, the allure of future returns equaling past performance was seductive.

"And, by the way," the speaker would say, "we have an x-million dollar minimum."

Well, now. This is sexy! This would be fun to tell your friends at a cocktail party. "Oh, I'm with Marble, Orchard, and Churchyard San Francisco. Yes, they have an x-million minimum and they have this unique approach that virtually guarantees…blah, blah, blah."

Then six weeks after the genius manager spoke, I'd receive an email newsletter from GPF management saying, "We are removing Marble, Orchard, and Churchyard from our platform due to recent poor performance. But never fear. We've replaced them with Coffin, Naylor, Paul, and Baer out of Boston. And they made 48% last year…" etcetera, ad infinitum.

So off we would go again.

Around this time, Google had begun to develop into a useful tool. (People forget there were years when Google was just one of many Internet search engines, a long way from the omnipresent force it is as I write this missive in 2012.)

I started doing a lot of Google searches on investing.

One thing I discovered is that every brokerage firm in every country recommends keeping most of your money in that country's securities and investing a bit of it in "foreign" securities. You would do well to know that there is a continental bias in the advice of most firms. But that's a topic for another day.

Much more important was my discovery of the "efficient-markets hypothesis" developed by Eugene Fama at the University Of Chicago Booth School Of Business.

Here's the quick definition from Wikipedia:

In finance, the efficient-markets hypothesis (EMH) asserts that financial markets are "informationally efficient." That is, one cannot consistently achieve returns in excess of average market returns on a risk-adjusted basis, given the information publicly available at the time the investment is made.

In other words, it is impossible for anyone to achieve an information edge.

For example, if you find out that a certain defense contractor will almost certainly receive a big order from a Middle Eastern country—and that order is likely to be approved by Congress—in a few seconds, everybody else will know it as well. In fact, forget about "in seconds"—we're talking microseconds. Subsequent trading in the market will automatically adjust the relevant security prices accordingly.

On the flip side, making a killing is always a tantalizing possibility. A cell phone maker beats out its rivals all because of the unexpected popularity of its offering phones in different colors. A hurricane threatens oil production in the Gulf of Mexico or unexpectedly wipes out the Florida orange juice crop. A little-known lab proves that "cold fusion" is a real, readily duplicable phenomenon. Some genius at a computer company discovers the equivalent of a way to get more angels to dance on the head of a pin.

You get the implications. If you're invested in the right instruments at the right time, you can still make enormous profits.

But that's not the important observation.

The important observation is: Has anybody made above-market return profits consistently, year after year after year over a statistically significant period of time?

The answer is "No!" It doesn't happen. Volumes of public data supporting this position are readily available to inquiring minds that want to know.

Relentless, Consistent Progress

The late Charley Lau was acknowledged as one of the greatest hitting coaches in all of baseball. He coached for Kansas City, the Yankees, the White Sox, and other major league teams. The *Wall Street Journal* even wrote about his "Ten Absolutes of Successful Hitting" in a front-page feature article.

Charley noted that baseball games are rarely won by home runs. Instead, they are won by the relentless run production of singles and doubles. They are won by batters who consistently hit the ball and hit into the whole field.

Sometimes, striving to hit a home run is essential. The problem is that it requires a batter to do about everything that's the opposite of what's required to simply hit the ball.

You have to make contact at the earliest possible second, which means far out in front of the plate. Then you have to contort your body to "pull" the ball instead of initiating a graceful, powerful follow-through that will drive the ball.

Fans pay for home runs, and when they occur, they are spectacular. There is no finer sight in baseball.

The problem is some batters strive to hit a home run each time they're at bat, whether a home run is necessary at that point or not. To say that ego gets in the way here is an understatement.

Charley Lau called this "the hero complex." He noted in the strongest possible terms how damaging it was to a given team's prospects.

"There should be a new statistic in baseball," Charley once said. "Instead of focusing on batting average, we should focus on 'runners advanced.' That's the true measure of a batter's skill, because the only way to achieve great numbers is to consistently hit the ball."

Does the Charley Lau philosophy apply to investing? I think it does.

The efficient-markets hypothesis—discrediting the likelihood of "hitting a home run" in the markets—is the first element of financial science and one of the things I found in my Google searches.

Another eye-opener I discovered is that the best estimate for tomorrow's stock price is today's stock price. Today's price represents an arm's length exchange between a willing buyer and a willing seller—with all information available to all parties.

Google searches also gave me references to the database of the Center for Research of Security Prices (CRSP) at the University of Chicago's Booth School of Business. I also found references to Dimensional Fund Advisors (DFA).

I learned about the Fama-French 3-Factor Model: stocks tend to outperform bonds over the long haul; small-cap stocks tend to outperform large-cap stocks over the long haul; and value stocks tend to outperform growth stocks over the long haul.

Additionally, I found an article that pitted Vanguard against DFA. Because both funds are so low-cost, the comparison comes up frequently. There are many differences and many similarities between DFA and Vanguard. For a detailed treatise, perform a Google search for "the best mutual funds: DFA or Vanguard?" and you will find information well beyond the scope of this manuscript.

I began to process what I'd been learning. Very quickly I found myself sitting in my office at the GPF, at age fifty-five, being asked to entice my friends to come and listen to presentations about things and by people that were not credible to me.

I became convinced that the genius stock-picking managers we were bringing in were fountains of financial pornography.

I don't know whether they knew it or not, but it didn't matter. I now thought they were wrong, wrong, wrong!

What turned me around was data.

There are two uniquely separate sources of information about the stock and bond markets: 1) the nearly mute voices of financial science and 2) the louder voice of the financial press with their financial pornography designed to seduce you to buy or sell securities or to sign over your money to some recently hot-handed investment manager or stockbroker.

What the vast majority of people are bombarded with is the louder voice of the financial press and, unfortunately, that's all they hear. Most people are never exposed to statistically significant historical data.

The statistically significant historical data is sobering. It cannot be explained away.

When do the market speculators ever have to account for any errors? "Ms. TV Investment Advisor, you said that there was every indication that the XYZ stock would soar by 50% over the next six months.

Well, we are now six months out, and XYZ has dropped in value by 35%. How do you explain your error?"

The explanation will never come. Or if it does, it will be some mush-mouthed litany about the unexpected rise in the price of gold, sunspots, and the fact that a Golden Monarch butterfly flapped its wings in China—and by the way, have you taken a look at our latest investment idea, the EFG company? Listen to this now, EFG has this unique, patent pending process for turning straw into gold. It's just awaiting EPA approval. But I can get you into it on the ground floor...

Please look at the data and decide for yourself.

Look at the actual performance figures.

Someone once said that the most treacherous phrase in an investor's vocabulary is, "This time it's different."

It is never different. Ever.

But greed springs eternal. Thus, GPF's brokers are with you always, "yea, even to the end of time." They are forever hyping the "latest new thing."

The more I looked at the data, the less I believed in the investment pornography I was being asked to put forward as part of my job. It got worse and worse until I realized that I had a first-class ethical dilemma on my hands. I no longer believed in what I was being asked to sell.

So I did the right thing—I quit.

I was extremely fortunate that I had enough wealth that I did not have to work.

But I wanted to do something interesting, something productive, and something I believed in. I decided to become a registered investment advisor and offer what I strongly believe to be the best option for stock and bond investors, Dimensional Fund Advisors (DFA).

DFA offers, in my humble opinion, mutual funds that capture the risk and reward factors of stocks and bonds in a manner that is superior to all others.

In addition to offering this superior investment option, I planned to be the low-cost provider of this optimal methodology.

Great idea, but it didn't work.

When I attempted to explain the methodology to people, they'd go to sleep. They'd be bored to tears. Something was missing, and I was certainly missing it.

I am constantly searching or "questing." One of my quests led me to a consultant who enlightened me as to what investors are really seeking—the achievement of personal goals. The scales fell from my eyes.

From my consultant, I learned that what was missing was simple. I can summarize it this way:

Investment management, while hugely important, is not what people of wealth are seeking.

What they are looking for is someone to help them identify and quantify their goals, values, needs, resources, and obligations and consultatively develop a plan that "buttons up" their wealth management in a comprehensive manner.

At a certain level, wealth is not about getting more wealth. It's about fulfilling personal goals with the tools at your unique personal disposal.

This was a revelation. It was a good fit since I enjoy listening to interesting folks.

Yes, I have a list of questions I ask during the discovery interview, but that list amounts to a broad, very loose set of inquiries. This is different from the traditional investment manager, who has been taught to ask a rigid list of questions designed to elicit a similarly rigid list of data points he or she can crank into a computer model supplied by a sponsoring firm to generate authoritative-sounding pronouncements.

I believe a wealth management firm should consult with clients, explore opportunities, visualize possibilities, take the time to get to know their clients, and help those clients identify their goals, values, needs, resources, and obligations.

In the final analysis, a wealth management firm should never sell anything. Rather, there should be a lot of listening, a lot of assessment, and, if it makes sense, an offer to help the prospective client achieve everything that is financially important to them.

DATA YOU CAN BELIEVE IN

In high school I had friends who were on the debate team. I bring this up because my buddies on the debate team alerted me to a particular book called *How to Lie with Statistics*. First published in 1954, this book by Darrell Huff shined a bright light on (according to Amazon.com), "…the slippery world of averages, correlations, graphs, and trends. Huff sought to break through 'the daze that follows the collision of statistics with the human mind.' The book remains relevant as a wake-up call for people unaccustomed to examining the endless flow of numbers pouring from Wall Street, Madison Avenue, and everywhere else [with] an axe to grind, a point to prove, or a product to sell."

When it comes to Wall Street and investment houses, anyone who owns a substantial number of mutual funds, stocks, and bonds will be painfully familiar with copious printed or online reports featuring indecipherable tables and charts.

Are they lying? No. Are they doing their level best to present a crystal-clear picture of their performance? Probably not, but who knows? That's just the point: Who knows?

So what can you as a goal-oriented investor do?

The answer is incredibly simple, but it is hidden from so many people. The answer is that you look at and trust data developed by academics over a long period of time—academics who have no financial interest in persuading you to invest in one thing or another; academics who have an instinct to "learn and share."

Please take a moment or three to let this sink in. Almost everything you see, read, hear, or view about investing—all the data and charts—is designed to persuade you to turn your money over to a given company and to pay that company the fees and commissions they charge.

Fees and commissions are your enemy. Of course, an advisor can't stay in business without charging something. I just want you to "know what good looks like" and pay the lowest fee possible while obtaining the most rational investment options available.

THE FINANCIAL SERVICES INDUSTRY WANTS YOUR MONEY

There are no exceptions. I don't care how it's pitched, couched, or phrased: the financial services industry wants your money and the fees that go with it.

The next time you are pitched an amazing sure thing, shake yourself by the shoulders, dunk your head in a bucket of cold water, and remind yourself, "If it sounds too good to be true, it is!" While you're drying your hair with your handkerchief, ask one point-blank question: "How much am I paying in commissions and fees for this opportunity?"

There are tens of thousands of licensed stockbrokers in this world, and they do not make a living by advising their clients to "buy and hold." Like that loveable E*TRADE baby, they make a living by persuading clients to buy and sell—to "trade"—securities.

The fact is that actively trading securities, actively chasing the next hot stock, is a loser's game. You do not have to believe me. Please, do your own research.

Analyze the objective data being served up by the academics and Nobel laureates. These folks are dedicated to learning as much as possible about the capital markets and to sharing that information.

The academics will challenge you to embrace financial science.

Financial science embraces four rather simple elements:

1. The efficient-markets hypothesis is closest to correct.
2. Risk and return are related.
3. Diversification reduces risk.
4. Portfolio structure explains performance.

Please do an Internet search on each of the above.

In a nutshell, financial science holds as its cornerstone the efficient-markets hypothesis, which asserts,

"It is unlikely that an investor will consistently achieve returns in excess of average market returns given the information available at the time the investment is made."

Point number two—that risk and return are related—addresses stocks versus bonds, small-cap stocks versus large-cap stocks, and value stocks versus growth stocks. The data revealed by researching the foregoing will lead most investors to a logical conclusion. The academic data is not trying to sell anything, but simply to provide an education.

For validation of point number three—diversification reduces risk—one need look no further than the fact that many high-flying securities have collapsed in value to zero. Investors could have owned a diversified portfolio of similar securities and likely not had their fender dented by the bankruptcy of the "high-flying darling of Wall Street" while still capturing the expected return of the sub-asset class.

Point number four—portfolio structure explains performance—is where the rubber meets the road for investors. The evidence of examining this point results in a firm conviction that investors should invest purposefully in a variety of sub-asset classes such that their unique personal goals are achieved.

At our company, we are happy to provide anybody who is curious with as much information about financial science and our investment philosophy as they desire. The data make a persuasive case.

If you want to gamble in the stock market—go for it.

If you want to achieve your unique personal goals—embrace financial science. This will put you well on the road to the essence of this chapter—smart investment decisions.

CHAPTER 5

MANAGING YOUR TAXES

When you *make* money, you have to *pay* money—to various branches of governments. So, it's not just how much you make, it's also how much you keep.

This is why investors can't focus solely on investment strategies and approaches.

Most folks know that our tax system—particularly at the federal level—is less than ideal. Most people also know that our system, as good as it is, will likely remain less than ideal for the foreseeable future.

So what can you do?

As with so many other aspects of wealth management, you can hire a specialist who is so knowledgeable that he or she can guide you in minimizing the amount of taxes you pay to the absolute minimum you legally owe.

WISDOM OF THE SAINTS

I'll never forget this nugget of wisdom from Saint Birgitta in the fourteenth century. "The Ten Commandments have been reduced to a single commandment: bring hither the money."

The blessed saint was referring to the church. But she might as well have been talking about our federal, state, and local governments.

Saint Birgitta may have been carrying things to extremes, but there can be no doubt that any authority endowed with the power to tax will use that power to the greatest extent that is politically feasible. "Bring hither the money!"

In the Middle Ages, that was about it. Today, we have CPAs and other tax professionals who say, "Not so fast..."

Actually, what the CPAs say to their clients is more like this: "You are making an investment in this or that. If we structure it this way, you'll pay a high rate of tax. On the other hand, if we structure it this other way the government will tax at a lower rate."

As a wealth management advisor, I can advise you as to whether a particular deal fits into your financial plan and, through consultation with my network of expert advisors, whether it is likely to be sound, but actually structuring such a deal for maximum tax efficiency is beyond my expertise.

Yet I know that it can be done, and I've seen it done.

I know CPAs who do it for my clients. That is the point of this chapter.

A CPA, NOT AN ACCOUNTANT

If you are a high net worth individual, you need a specialist, and that usually means a specialist CPA, not just an accountant.

You need somebody who makes a point of staying absolutely current with the tax law in your area or areas of enterprise and of investment—someone who understands the nuances of the complex.

I'm convinced that things are unlikely to change. You are always going to need a good CPA to handle your taxes.

As there are specialists in other professions, there are CPAs who specialize in specific areas. It's crucial for you to understand the special niche of your CPA or of the CPA with whom you may eventually choose to work.

As there are physicians who specialize in pediatrics or neurosurgery, there are CPA specialists for household tax filings and there are CPAs who are specialists in incredibly complex corporate finances and a myriad of situations in between.

There are CPAs who know everything about the tax considerations implicit with oil and gas and "intangible drilling costs." There are others who stay on top of regional rules, tax credits for historic buildings, and other nuances. In my marketplace, there is a lot of land that, due to being located in a registered historic district, is eligible for preferential tax treatment if you build on it; hence, we have a number of local CPAs who are experts in that field.

So, given that not all CPAs are alike and that they each have their areas of specialty, it's important to have the right CPA.

A Wide Variability in Pricing

Some CPAs charge by the hour, so the greater their expertise in relevant areas, the less time they'll have to spend researching and the lower your bill.

I've also known of at least one CPA, however, who apparently charges based on the income of his clients. For example, one client of mine reports earned income in the range of $600,000 a year. This CPA was charging him an exorbitant $6,000 a year to do his taxes, which is 1% of his gross income. I learned this when I was conducting the discovery interview with my prospective client and asking questions like, "Who's your CPA?" "Are you dealing with him because you like him?" "Is he or she a family member?" "Is he or she a fraternity brother or sorority sister?" "Are you dealing with your CPA out of habit or do you know that this CPA possesses vast expertise in your niche?"

Be assured that we are not trying to blow up professional or personal relationships and we're not trying to get people to fire their current advisors. In fact, if a client has a CPA, we will often call (with our mutual client's consent) to make the CPA aware of things we're aware of regarding the client. We want to help our clients' advisors be as good as they can be. We want to help our clients advisors serve our mutual client to maximum advantage.

An excellent example of our working with an existing CPA is the case of one of our retired clients who was faced with the decision of taking withdrawals either from her IRA or from her taxable accounts. We met with the CPA and determined a tax-advantaged blended distribution from both the IRA and the taxable account that would keep our client in a lower tax bracket.

In the case of the client with the CPA who charged based on the total income, the client said that he was with this CPA "kind of out of habit." He advised that the CPA was winding down his practice and was not responsive to phone calls or emails. Further, this client didn't particularly like the CPA. He said there was nothing political keeping him in the relationship, and he wanted me to introduce him to a few other people.

As we understood the complexity of his financial affairs—which was pretty much W-2 income, mortgage interest, and some charitable donations—we were able to engage a CPA who did this client's annual tax returns for $175. Wow, no longer $6,000 per year— just $175 per year. Saving over $5,800 annually is beneficial to most folks!

The lesson here is to regularly perform due diligence on your advisors, their performance, and, of course, what you're paying them.

GREATER COMPLEXITY, MORE SPECIAL EXPERTISE

The affairs of most high net worth individuals are much more complex. They might own a divided or undivided interest in a number of different enterprises, which could be real estate, oil and gas, or widget factories. They could have all kinds of charitable interests. They might be thinking about setting up a family foundation, where they would get a specific deduction if they create a foundation (30%) and a different, more attractive, deduction (50%) if they create a donor advised fund.

Your CPA will—in a best-case scenario—be familiar with the requirements for entities like donor advised funds, charitable remainder trusts and family limited partnerships. Hopefully, he or she will be proactive and will come to you with ideas. For your part, in my opinion, you should be visiting with your CPA at least every six months, not only at tax time.

In fact, a great CPA is not somebody who merely takes your tax documents and processes them. A great CPA takes the time to sit down and consult with you to understand any financial changes that have occurred in your life since your last meeting.

Here's a good example of the kinds of things a proactive CPA might suggest. Let's assume that you project a major increase in income for the year. That means you'll be paying more in taxes. Your CPA might suggest that you purchase some tax credits for, often, as little as eighty cents on the dollar.

In Oklahoma, when a bank makes qualified loans, it gets state tax credits. The bank then owns these tax credits. The banks may actually give these tax credits away as an incentive to customers and clients. But at the end of the year, it may decide to sell its inventory of such credits. I was asked to do just that when I worked for a bank.

The credits were priced—in quantity—for eighty cents on the dollar. If someone had to pay state income tax of $100,000, that $100,000 worth of state tax credits might be purchased for $80,000 or even less. Now that's beneficial!

This is one example of the kinds of things a good CPA can do to help clients. (By the way, selling dollar bills for eighty cents each in quantity was pretty easy sledding!)

IS IT A MATCH?

As I have said, we are definitely not out to interfere with established professional relationships. However, if a client doesn't have a CPA or is in any way dissatisfied with his or her current relationship, I will always attempt to match him or her with someone who can best serve that client's needs.

And I do mean *match*.

As with any advisor, it's not solely about expertise. It's also about chemistry. Life is too short to endure uncomfortable relationships. So if I observe a need for one of my clients, I'm going to say, "Mr. or Mrs. Client, you're the CEO, I'm your CFO, and I have observed an opportunity to enhance..."

This happened recently. I have a long-time client, a very wealthy man, who is fascinated by tax law. He does his own taxes and thoroughly enjoys it. I suggested to him that we engage someone who is a full-time CPA to give him a second opinion and review his tax filing documents to see if there were any opportunities for enhancement. I didn't see a problem with what he was doing already, but I'm a perfectionist. I wanted to look for more opportunities to move the ball down the field. No one should have to pay a cent more in tax than what the law requires—unless they want to. Tax law is complex. Getting a second opinion is clearly the smart move.

I tend to have a fondness for small, specialized firms—CPA, law office, insurance firms, etc.—versus large operations.

There are large firms that offer everything from a family mission statement to arranging a loan at a favorable rate. In my experience these firms can be like Swiss army knives in their approach—they do a little bit of everything but nothing really well.

My preference is for a drawer full of discrete, specialized tools, if you will. Now I don't have all of those resources in my office, but I certainly know a large number of the best people in my market.

"YOU HAVE THE RIGHT TO A CPA"

It probably shouldn't be this way, but if the IRS or other tax authority comes in to see you, *do not talk to them*. The only thing you should give them is the name and contact information for your CPA. If you do not follow this advice, you may innocently say something that you don't have the expertise to discuss. (I know this from painful personal experience!)

The situation is similar to insisting on your right to an attorney should law enforcement ever come to call. (Mercifully, this is not something I know about from personal experience!)

MORE ON SMALL SHOPS

As most folks are aware, the deal that people make regarding employment is this: I will show up every day, on time, dressed to play. In return, you will pay me a wage and benefits, including a certain amount of vacation time. (Mutual loyalty used to be part of the deal, but that largely went away a long time ago.)

The deal means that, unless you're in sales, you won't have to "hunt" each day. You come in, do your work, and go home, and every two weeks you get a check. Oh, and you will do what your supervisor tells you to do. You will abide by the rules set by the corporate bureaucracy, and the company will determine your income.

Now, I ask you: Do you think that the very best professionals—CPAs, attorneys, wealth management advisors, etc.—work on these terms? Would the very best people agree to this deal? Maybe they would when they're young and learning the ropes. But as they measure themselves against their peers and become aware of the market demand for their intellectual capital, the very best will, quite often (not always), go out on their own.

I've got the perfect example. It's my old buddy from Grand Lake, Tony. Tony was a geologist, and he got a job with an oil and gas firm right out of college.

After the first week, Tony went to the owner and said he had all kinds of ideas on how to do things better and how the company could make a lot more money. The owner was indulgent, but ultimately said, "Tony, just go back to your office and do your job. We'll talk about all this in a couple of years."

Later that day the boss was walking past Tony's office and saw him filling a great big cardboard box with his stuff.

"Tony, what are you doing?"

"I'm leaving," Tony said. "If you don't want to embrace great ideas, I'm going to go out and start my own firm. You can't talk me out of it."

It was a very brash move, and Tony might not have done it if he'd had a family to support at the time. But he went out and started his own firm that same afternoon. Reflecting, at the end of a hard day on the lake, he would proudly say that he'd only received one paycheck in his life, and that was for his one week working for that firm.

People who are good and know it don't even think there's a possibility of them failing. They say, "This is what I want to do. This is going to enrich my life in many ways." Then, with a lot of hard work and a large measure of good fortune, they accidentally make a lot of money, too (maybe).

I am by no means suggesting that good people are immune to failure. I'm also not saying that large firms are devoid of talent. I'm saying that you should consider small boutique firms when you are looking for a truly talented professional advisor.

TAX TIP

Finally, most people don't realize that what CPAs charge for a given service can be seasonal.

Here's a decent "private deal" example. Suppose you own an apartment complex and you sell 80% of it to a syndicate of private investors. You get a lump sum of cash, and the syndicate investors get a portion of future net operating income and their share of future depreciation.

In most cases, you would be required to send your investors (and the IRS) a K-1 reporting a variety of financial details. This is a statutory form that must be filed, and you'll probably want your CPA to handle it. But you may be able to control when the form is filed. Therein exists an opportunity to get the work done for less.

The busiest time of the year for a CPA is, quite naturally, between January 1 and April 15. Their slow period is from April 15 through mid-summer with their schedules getting busy again as the calendar approaches October 15, the final filing date. Many CPAs cut their rates during this period.

This is why many professional deal syndicators— private equity firms come to mind—often delay issuing

K-1's so that their taxes get done in June, July, and August, at a lower, preferential billing rate.

I realize that everyone doesn't have a property to sell to a deal syndicator. In fact, this little bit of information about K-1 forms and preferential CPA billing rates is not my point. My point is simply this: High net worth individuals, ideally in concert with their wealth management advisors, should be proactive when it comes to working with their CPAs or any other advisor.

Don't just go with the flow. Ask questions. Be candid and complete in the information you share. Help them to help you.

Managing your taxes is easier with the right CPA advising you and is as intuitively beneficial as the old adage "a penny saved is a penny earned."

CHAPTER 6

ESTATE PLANNING: RUNNING THE WORLD FROM THE GRAVE

Where do your assets go after you die?

This is the question at the heart of estate planning. There are many other questions as well, but that's the main one.

Estate planning is vital for everyone, regardless of wealth.

There are certain legal instruments that absolutely everyone should have in place. But for the vast—the very vast—majority of citizens, estate planning is not complicated.

If you're "rich," things are different. Calculating the number of millionaires in the United States is tricky, but a reasonable estimate places the number at around 7.8 million households. That's out of an estimated total of 115 million households, for an estimated total of nearly 7%.

Unfortunately, today, if you have $1 million in net worth, you're not really rich. You're wealthier than 93% of the other households in the country, and by many standards, you are a high net worth individual. But you're not *rich* rich.

Do the arithmetic. For example, let's say you have three children and a spouse. You die, then your spouse dies, and your estate is ready to be distributed—but not until your executor has forked over a significant amount in accountant fees, legal fees, miscellaneous fees, and possibly estate taxes.

When everything has been sorted out and all the taxes and fees paid, each of your three children might get their share.

Let's assume that estate settlement costs are minimal and each child gets $325,000. That might pay for college educations for your grandchildren if they go to state schools, but it's not going to endow a wing at a major art museum or other institution. In fact, it's not going to endow anything. Maybe your children could use it to pay down their mortgages?

If, on the other hand, your net worth is north of $5 million, you might want to consider a different approach. You might want to leave a certain amount to each of your children and leave the rest to a family foundation or other charitable entity.

The greater your net worth, the greater the number of possibilities you have. Only you are in the unique position to deal with this, and I encourage you to make the decisions now.

It doesn't matter whether you're worth a million, five million, or a hundred million—it is your privilege and responsibility, in my view, to make *purposeful* arrangements for what happens to your wealth when you're gone.

I have said this before: It is every citizen's duty to pay whatever taxes he or she legally owes, but not a penny more.

The same applies to estate taxes.

This is why: regardless of your net worth, you need a specialist estate planning attorney. You need an expert.

So many times we discover that our clients are working with a particular attorney out of habit. As with CPAs, many clients choose their attorneys based on personal relationships—college schoolmate, family member, a recommendation from a good friend, or so on.

That's how business goes, I know. But when you're talking about wealth management, we recommend you choose your advisors based on demonstrated professional competence and personal chemistry.

If estate planning is the issue, you don't want an attorney who does a little divorce law, a little criminal or civil law, and the occasional traffic ticket or real estate closing. You will be best served by a professional specialist who is passionate about estate planning. I want my clients to be served by someone who is fascinated by estate tax law and has a compulsion to stay up-to-date.

Legal generalists surely have their place. But they are, probably, not the most knowledgeable professionals to prepare your estate planning documents.

THE FOUR PRIMARY ELEMENTS OF AN ESTATE PLAN

Every estate plan should include the following four elements:

- Marital deduction trust or personal trust
- Pour-over will
- Advance directive
- Durable power of attorney

Marital Deduction Trust or Personal Trust. It is important to hold your assets in a trust like this because it will enable your spouse and/or executors to avoid going through probate and all manner of other inconvenient tedium upon your death. I won't mince words here: Probating a will delays the flow of the proceeds to the surviving beneficiaries, often by many months or years. In addition, probate proceedings are public information and they are expensive.

Pour-Over Will. This is a will that makes sure that any assets not already in your trust at the time of your death will automatically be "poured" over into your trust. This document won't always work, but, in my view it's worth having in place.

Advance Directive. This is a legal document that says, "If I'm incapacitated, these are my instructions to my family and physicians." Basically, it tells people to either pull the plug if your health has deteriorated to a state that you've defined or use extraordinary means to keep you alive if your health has deteriorated to a state that, again, you've defined.

I am not an attorney, but I know from personal experience that the hospital is ultimately in charge, regardless of what your advance directive says. Someone very near and dear to me had a massive stroke. Her advance directive said, in effect, "Pull the plug." But the sisters at this Catholic hospital told me candidly, "If the patient is alive four days from now, we're going to hook her up to all kinds of life support machines."

One would like to think that this is a moral decision on the part of the hospital. But I'll speculate, with no disrespect meant, that it's more about avoiding liability.

Durable Power of Attorney. This legal document makes sure that if you're out of the country or if you're incapacitated, a person you appoint can conduct business on your behalf. Usually that means paying bills and handling your money.

The aforementioned are "the big four" for just about everybody, regardless of level of wealth. But once you get into relatively greater wealth, heirs, and holdings, opportunities present themselves. With those opportunities, things become more complicated and require the services of an expert.

THE BIG "NO FOLLOW THROUGH" PROBLEM

Here's an incredible fact. Time and time again I've seen many individuals accept expert advice and enlist the services of a wonderful estate-planning attorney. They get everything set up. All the structures and trust "containers" are in place. Then the client fails to fund the trusts! They do not actually transfer the assets and funds that are part of the plan into the various "trust containers."

Why? I have no idea.

I have no idea why people take the time and trouble to consult with a skilled estate planning lawyer to set up trusts, then leave the office saying, "Oh, I'll take care of that," when asked about actually funding the trusts they've created. Then they never do it. You cannot imagine how many times this happens. This means all their planning and legal work is for naught. Why not have the estate planning attorney prepare all the documents to do the funding, so the client only has to sign a few more forms and the attorney executes everything? My attorney changed title to my property for me, including bank accounts, brokerage accounts, real estate, and a myriad of other private deal assets.

I do have a speculation about why this happens so often. I can offer a real-life example. I was once at a breakfast meeting in a private hotel conference room with a wealthy individual and about six other people involved in a particular deal.

The client had paid the hotel to lay out its standard breakfast spread: cold cereal, milk, Danish pastries, fresh bread, scrambled eggs, bacon, coffee, tea, and— you know the drill.

The client was a former hedge fund manager, and I'd guess he was all of forty-five years old. I'd also guess he was worth over $100 million. Yet at the meeting, several times, he complained about how much this breakfast spread and room rental had cost. At another point he said to one of the participants, "You're young, and I'm rich."

Leave aside the man's complete lack of manners. My point is that the wealthy can be as cost conscious, or even more so, than any person who doesn't have much money.

Being able to enjoy your money is not directly correlated with how much money you have. When it comes to actually funding the trusts they have paid a top-flight attorney to create, humans often cheap out and—to save the billable hours—say they will handle it themselves. Then they don't!

Madness? You be the judge.

PLAYING THE WHOLE BALLGAME

Don't fall into the trap of not funding your trusts. I don't care how much you're worth. We strongly urge everyone to let the estate planning attorney who has drawn up your plan play the whole game and handle the funding of the trusts you've set up.

As the client, you should not opt to pitch the final inning yourself. Indeed, I would say, "What on earth are you thinking of?" Let the attorney do it, pay him or her any additional fee, and sleep well at night knowing that it's done.

Once you get your estate plan done, you don't have to visit with your estate planning attorney as often as you visit your dentist. But laws and situations are constantly changing, so you should see him or her and review your plan on a regular basis—no less than every five years, even for only a cursory review.

EVENT-DRIVEN PLAN REVIEWS

There is also the event-driven review. Events can be things like: you inherit money, you have a new child, a beneficiary dies, or, heaven forbid, your wealth takes a turn for the worse.

I often refer to my clients as the matriarch and/or patriarch of their family, and often they are the wealth creators. It's not unusual for them to have beneficiaries. They need to make individualized decisions about their beneficiaries (sons, daughters, grandkids). Some say, "I'm giving each one an equal share. That's how it's always been done."

I've also seen situations where the matriarch and/or patriarch will say, "My oldest son has never demonstrated fiscal responsibility, so when I die, I want his portion of my estate to be used to purchase a lifetime annuity. He'll get a check every month for the rest of his life, and he can't invade the corpus."

I've also witnessed scenarios where they say, "My second daughter has never earned a dime in her life. She's never held a real job. So, I will make a two-for-one offer. If she can demonstrate that she has earned $30,000 in a year, she can bring the evidence in to the trustee, and they will write her a check for $60,000."

Of course, selectivity of this sort can blow up. What if one of your kids becomes a brain surgeon while the other one feels a calling to become a missionary in Africa? The two siblings are going to have a huge disparity in income.

So someone, the trustee, needs to have some latitude to make certain specified decisions upon the death of the matriarch or patriarch.

YOU NEED A CORPORATE TRUSTEE

This is where families can benefit by having a corporate trustee.

You need someone who specializes in it, not some brother-in-law who once worked at a bank. Again, specialization is the key. A corporate trustee will be able to administer tough love and also the laws governing wills and estates. They are trained to do this. They have special training, liability insurance, and lawyers behind them to help them interpret the documents. It eliminates family entanglements and family-based requests.

In other words, you may need an impartial third-party trust administrator and/or trustee. You don't want to set up a situation where Uncle Fred is in charge, and one of the relatives comes to him screaming, "Uncle Fred, this just isn't fair!" If that happens, Uncle Fred may feel pressured to unravel your carefully crafted plan or risk major intra-family unhappiness.

I've seen cases of family members who were trustees actually resign because they couldn't stand the pressure. Then one of the family-member beneficiaries comes back to Uncle Fred and yells, "Even in the thirty days you had authority over the account, you could have done this and that for me!"

WHERE TO LOOK FOR A TRUSTEE

In my experience, trust companies are a great place to start the search for a qualified corporate trustee.

Another benefit of utilizing a trust company is that they will "silo" an estate's assets, unlike, say a brokerage firm, where the securities are held in the firm's "street name." This "silo" feature provides another level of protection against asset dissipation.

A good, thoughtful corporate trustee will provide extraordinary services. They might even walk your dog. They may stand by your side and help you make funeral arrangements, even to the point of helping you pick out a dress for Grandma to be buried in.

A Rainbow of Trust Possibilities

As I mentioned in a previous chapter, I have one client who is simply fascinated by tax law and insists on doing his own taxes (though I've repeatedly advised him to get a second opinion from a good CPA).

Trusts and estates, however, are such a complex area, particularly if you are a high net worth individual, that you have no business trying to do it yourself.

For example, should you have a revocable or an irrevocable trust? Or if you are in a profession where you might be sued, should you have all your assets in your spouse's name? What about an asset protection trust (available in some states)? Or an irrevocable life insurance trust (ILIT)? What if you own property in several different states?

You need experts to help and guide you, not attorneys who do a little of this and a little of that.

HOW A WEALTH MANAGER CAN HELP

When it comes to estate planning, a wealth manager can be of enormous help in two ways. First, he or she can help you find an estate planning attorney who is simpatico with you and your personality.

Second, a wealth manager can make the process more efficient. For example, whenever I meet with the attorney a client has selected, I do what in the computer world is called a "core dump." I give him or her everything I've learned about the client's wealth, holdings, and estate-planning goals.

In other words, I condense what may have been four hours of client interviews into about fifteen minutes of key data. I can do this because estate planning attorneys and I speak a similar language when it comes to assets, and, as a wealth manager, I know much of what they need to know.

Typically, there will be an opening chat with the client, the attorney, possibly the attorney's associates—who charge less and will be doing the heavy lifting—and me. We'll deal with high level concepts and broad goals.

Then the attorney will take the stage. I will sit back and listen. The attorney will make a presentation of his or her ideas and suggestions on what we should do to move forward.

When he finishes, I'll jump back in and say, "Based on what you understand now, what is this going to cost and how long will it take? Are you going to do all this work yourself, or are you going to farm it out to one of your assistants?"

Some questions my client might not feel comfortable asking. "What is your bill rate? What is your legal assistant's bill rate? Do you charge a set fee or charge separately for transferring assets into the trust?"

I am not an estate planning expert. But I do know many of the right questions to ask. As a third party, I serve as my client's advocate.

CONCLUSION

As I write this, the federal estate tax situation is completely up in the air. No one knows what the exemption and tax rate will be in the future because Congress has failed to act.

Congress will act eventually, of course. But as it acts, it will also almost certainly add more loopholes and "gotchas" on top of previously established law.

There is also a movement to eliminate the "death tax" completely. After all, through an objective lens, the estate tax amounts to double taxation since the deceased has already paid tax on anything left in his or her estate. But then, there has always been such a movement.

Experience would indicate that the movement to repeal the estate tax has about as much chance as when pigs fly. If you are a high net worth individual, the need has never been greater to have a top-flight estate planning attorney on your side. That is never going to change.

Running the world from the grave is your privilege and responsibility, at least as it relates to the disposition of your accumulated net assets.

CHAPTER 7

PROTECTING YOUR WEALTH WITH CONSULTATIVE RISK MANAGEMENT

For most people, insurance is about what the law requires for your car, making sure you can rebuild your house should it burn down, and replacing items should they be lost or stolen.

That's true for people of wealth as well. But if you have money and assets, you have other issues, not the least of which is liability.

In my view insurance protects and/or, in the case of life insurance, creates wealth.

When it comes to insurance, the primary things are your home, your autos, and any personal possessions.

Attendant with home and auto insurance is liability insurance. So if somebody slips and falls in your front yard and breaks an elbow, then your liability kicks in. That's usually sufficient for most people.

But not for the wealthy!

Everyone has liability concerns, of course, but for high net worth individuals it is a much greater concern than for most. This is for one reason: They are high net worth individuals.

In other words, there's money there, for plaintiffs and especially for lawyers.

LAW OF THE JUNGLE

I know there are completely legitimate liability cases, and I don't want to minimize that fact. But too often with liability cases, I feel like I'm watching a Jane Goodall documentary about chimpanzees. One chimp is fortunate enough to locate a bunch of bananas. Or maybe that chimp works for it, climbing a tree, gnawing off the stem, and so forth. Another chimp takes notice and says, in effect, "I want that. Give it to me—or else."

We may call ourselves "civilized," but the law of the jungle still applies. Genetically, human beings and chimps are between 95 and 98.5% identical. You can make of that what you will, but at the plaintiff's bar, it seems to mostly come down to "you've got it, I want it, give me that."

THE BIGGEST GAP

The biggest gap we see when people come into our office—maybe they have suddenly become wealthy, sold a business, had a "liquidity event," or they slowly became wealthy over time by earning and being frugal—is that these folks do not have a *personal umbrella policy*. (A personal umbrella policy is an "excess liability" policy that sits on top of your home and auto.)

You may have home insurance with a $1 million liability and auto with a $500,000 liability. If you are a person of means, you would be wise to add an umbrella for $1, $3, or $5 million on top of all that.

Not to do so is to be penny wise and pound foolish.

Many of our clients have been able to get a $5 million umbrella for a premium of about $450 a year. That's on the order of a dollar a day. For a $5 million policy! Considering the alternative, who wouldn't be willing to pay $450 a year for that kind of protection?

But here's a reality check. What most people don't realize is that this policy is not only in place to pay for damages. This policy is going to pay a whole bunch of lawyers to defend you and the insurance company (which will have the privilege of ultimately writing a check) before any judgment is rendered or paid.

When someone sues you—events begin to unfold, the "victims" contact a lawyer, the lawyer discovers that you have considerable resources and he wants them—the lawyer may actually get a third or more of the amount of the judgment. The insurance company underwriting your personal umbrella policy therefore will make it very expensive for said lawyer to pursue the case and eliminate a lot of aggravation for you—the insured.

Should the plaintiff's attorney lawsuit for damages exceed the limits of your auto and home liability, the insurance company that issued your umbrella policy is going to expend a terrific amount of time and energy with their own in-house lawyers before they're ever going to write anybody a check. Tort attorneys know this.

PITY THE POOR TORT ATTORNEY—NOT!

The attorney representing the "victims" knows that he or she can sue you for $15 million and perhaps even get a favorable judgment. But will you pay? What if you refuse to write them a check? Just because somebody sues you and wins a judgment, it doesn't mean you'll be forced, or able, to pay them.

So pity the poor tort attorney. He has risked his time, which is the only capital he has, to win a judgment against you.

Fairness isn't the issue. He's won. You refuse or aren't able to pay. Now, the attorney has his client who brought the suit call up saying, "Where's my money? I need that cash!" Of course, the attorney doesn't get his one-third cut until the funds flow. Now can we pity both of them?

My point about your need for an excess liability umbrella policy is that it is a dangerous and complex world out there if you have money. There are attorneys cruising for high-value targets. (Not for nothing are some attorneys likened to ambulance chasers.) You don't even have to consult huge ads in your local Yellow Pages to verify this. Simply turn on the TV. "Have you been injured? [Or been exposed to asbestos or taken a given drug or whatever...] You may be entitled to compensation. Contact us at 800-555-XXXX."

I do not in any way want to minimize the gravity of the issue, but, ladies and gentlemen, in the end, this is largely a zero-sum game where one party wins at the expense of the other.

That means, "I pit my wits, resources, and strategies against yours." If you're an attorney, your "inventory" is your time. How much of it do you want to expend? How much do you want to risk? (Don't forget the overhead of operating your office.)

Payments can be delayed indefinitely. So, imagine this conversation between the plaintiff's attorney and your insurance company, "Yes, you obtained a judgment against us for $7 million, and we're going to fight it. But how about this: Here's a check for $1 million right here and now. Will you take it and go away?"

It is definitely not pretty. But this is the way it is. Attorneys will do everything they can to pierce your insurance barriers, and insurance companies will do everything they can to defend against such assaults. After all, you've paid the premium, and they're on the hook for the payment. But it's in their best interests to keep the money in their pocket as long as possible and to write as small a check as possible.

Did I say it's a game? It's more like a blood sport. I wish things were otherwise, but they're not, so you need an umbrella liability policy of purposeful size.

THE WEALTHY DON'T DO "RETAIL"

I know many high net worth individuals, including a handful of billionaires. I've observed that they are not buying insurance online or going down to the insurance office in their local strip mall. The companies they deal with may not even be visible to the typical man on the street. The companies serving them don't advertise on TV or elsewhere because their target clientele is so limited that a mass medium doesn't benefit them in any way.

We endeavor to get our clients the level of insurance service and options appropriate to their financial stature. Only rarely can such needs be met by retail, mass-market insurance companies. The majority of our clients are best served by institutional-level insurance services.

The purpose of insurance is to protect your resources and your assets. Your resources may include not only your various investments and the businesses you own; they may also include your intellectual capital. You may have homes all over the world, jewelry, artwork, and exotic assets like wine collections, vintage guitars, baseball cards, antique cars, luxury boats, or private planes, to name a few exotic assets that a standard policy is not designed to cover.

You need highly personalized and consultative service. You don't need a salesman trying to win a trip to Hawaii. The professionals who operate at this higher level specialize in serving wealthy clients with complex needs. Their practices tend to be driven more through referral than by marketing and selling their services. They don't run ads in newspapers.

What this means to you is that finding these consultative risk managers is something of a trick. The most fruitful approach is likely to be asking other high net worth individuals for suggestions—or locate a firm that specializes in serving the wealthy.

UNDER THE SAME ROOF

Once you find a professional who specializes in offering institutional-level insurance services, someone you like, I urge you to move all of your insurance coverage to a single agent and a single underwriting company to the extent possible. It's much easier to get the full attention of a service provider when your relationship with them is of substantial mass.

You will almost certainly receive a discount for concentrating your business. But more importantly, when all of your policies are with a single company, there's no other company at which the insurer can point a finger. In fact, I like to say, "No one can point fingers, they've only got thumbs. Those thumbs can only be used to gesture to their chest in a motion that everyone knows stands for, 'It's me on the hook.'"

When something happens, it doesn't matter whether it is covered by your homeowners, car, or umbrella. There is no room for debate. If you have all of your coverage with the same company, then that company is on the hook for any insurance-related issues. Further, your consultative risk management professional will be right in the middle of resolving the dilemma.

INSURANCE ADVISORS

Now, what about that insurance advisor? You want someone who is going to meet with you and spend a lot of time getting to know you and the inventory of what you have, the risks of owning it, who owns it, and how you own it. He or she will identify all of the bizarre risks that you may be exposed to such that all needs are identified, the coverage fits together without gaps, and there's nothing out there dangling. Then, when your house burns down, and yes, you did happen to have a priceless Picasso hanging in your living room, it is covered, no question.

You want someone who is very, very thorough.

In all likelihood, someone from the insurance company— undoubtedly a specialist—will visit you at your home and have you show him or her your personal possessions. This is no time to be secretive or shy. You want your insurance company to know about all of your valuable possessions.

BUSINESS INSURANCE

We've also got to talk about business insurance, and for a very simple reason: The wealth of many people is directly tied to the business or businesses they own. Compared to homeowners, auto, and liability, business insurance represents an entirely different set of critters.

Here's an example of how different business-related insurance can be. Let's say you own a manufacturing company that you want to sell. This is where a good insurance advisor will say, "Good. So you manufacture widgets. What happens if you sell your company and a year from now someone who bought a widget when you owned the company sues you because his or her widget blew up and took off his or her hand? You're liable for that. The person who bought the company is going to say, 'We didn't own the company then. You need to go back to the previous owner.'"

PURPOSEFUL WEALTH MANAGEMENT

When you sell a company you should consider procuring "tailing liability insurance." Such policies can be designed to cover you for ten or more years after you sell your firm.

This is not an abstract example. For many years, I owned an industrial valve sales and service company. My company repaired a valve for a refinery in New Mexico. I sold this company in 1997. In 1999 or 2000, there was a fire at the refinery and they claimed the cause was a valve repaired by Warburton Valve in 1996. The people who bought my company from me called and said, "Tom, there's a problem—and it's your problem."

Fortunately, I had purchased tailing liability insurance, so I didn't have to worry about it.

Why did I purchase this insurance? I had a very good insurance advisor who made me aware of risks I'd not properly considered.

This is the kind of foresight and service I am referring to when I speak of institutional-level insurance delivered via consultation.

MY MOST MEMORABLE INSURANCE CHALLENGE

It may be that "memorable" is not quite accurate, but this challenge was certainly unusual, even for someone like me who specializes in providing a family-office wealth management experience. I have two clients who enjoy volunteer police work. Their volunteer work involves "strapping iron." I think they carry Glock 40mm semi-automatic pistols.

For those readers on the two coasts, I should add that Oklahoma is sometimes fairly viewed as the Wild West. We have different attitudes about guns. In fact, you can buy ammunition in some grocery stores, though, for the time being, you have to leave your "piece" in the car.

My two clients don't know each other, but they share a common interest and do volunteer police work. As things have turned out, they can afford to donate their services. The challenge developed that it was impossible to find any company who would provide any excess liability umbrella on these men through normal channels. The insurance companies are all afraid the guy's going to go out and shoot somebody by mistake or by intent and that it won't be covered by the municipality's insurance. So the claim would come back to each firm as personal liability. Nobody wanted to write these policies.

It took some effort, but I finally found, through special markets, a company that would write insurance for volunteer cops.

It sounds like I'm blowing my own horn here—but it's actually the horn of my network of expert insurance advisors.

It is crucial to be aware that solutions exist; you just need the right person to find them.

LIFE INSURANCE

Property, casualty, and liability insurance are more or less discrete disciplines. Life insurance is a totally different animal.

It may very well be that your property and casualty insurance company won't offer life insurance. Therefore, you won't be able to bring all of your coverage under the same roof.

A competent wealth management advisor will explain why you might or might not need life insurance. In my view the benefits of life insurance are numerous, including: 1) it provides "over the top" money for the surviving spouse (if any), 2) whole life insurance builds cash value that can serve as a safety net if other assets are exhausted, 3) life insurance increases the value of an estate for the benefit of heirs, 4) life insurance is received tax free and can be used to pay estate taxes, 5) the cash value in life insurance is currently exempt from judgments, 6) and a myriad of other reasons I will elaborate on later.

The "flavors" of life insurance are finite but available in a variety of forms. A thorough wealth management advisor will be able to explain your options in plain English and often solicit bids from a number of life insurance salespeople to make sure you get the best deal and have chosen a purposeful course of action.

Full disclosure: I have my license to sell life insurance in the state of Oklahoma, though I've never sold a policy. I went to the classes and took the test to get that license to find out from the inside how the industry works. Sure enough, as soon as my new qualifications were announced, my email inbox was inundated with messages from companies who said, in effect, "If you sell some of this policy, you'll win a trip to Hawaii and/or benefit from our currently greatly increased commission schedule."

The motivations for life insurance salespeople to sell product are immense and sometimes in conflict with the needs of the insured. In my experience, it is more difficult to find life insurance agents who work as fiduciaries for their clients than any other profession. I'm disappointed that my experience has revealed to me that too many life insurance salespeople are just selling stuff for the companies that offer the best sales incentives. In lieu of the foregoing, I do want to go on record as saying that I know a number of highly consultative life insurance sales agents who do a terrific job for their clients. These are the agents I get my clients in front of.

A salesperson is not what we're looking for. What we're looking for is someone who can offer *purposeful* life insurance. The key is to find an agent who has a predisposition to want to be helpful and who is not driven solely by his or her personal profit motive.

Again, a skilled wealth manager can connect you with the highest order of life insurance professionals.

A WORD ABOUT ANNUITIES

Speaking of life insurance and planning for the future, the humorist (and my fellow Oklahoman) Will Rogers famously said he never met a man he didn't like. Well, I've rarely met an annuity that I do like.

In fact, there's an adage in the financial services industry that suggests annuities are never purchased, they're only sold. This means that no one goes shopping for annuities. The annuity sales force comes to the customer.

The concept of an annuity sounds wonderful, on paper. You pay a company a certain amount of money, and some years later, they start paying you an amount of money each month until you die.

There are tax implications, there are insurance implications, and every annuity policy has its own restrictions.

For example, suppose you invest in an annuity, and they guarantee an 8% return in ten years. But when that date arrives, you can't get the money. They say they will convert it into an income stream, for you, or for your wife, or for whoever is the first to die, or whatever. X number of years, with a Y-year guarantee on terms they dictate at that time! But, importantly, they may not be willing to actually give you the money because the annuity has promised a "notional" future value as opposed to an "actual" future value.

In other words, the distribution options on annuities are very complex. In my view, you need somebody to help you sort through them other than the insurance person. You need an independent advisor.

Let's not forget sales commissions. Let's suppose you buy an annuity contract for $100,000. The selling agent's commission may total as much as $13,000. He or she may not care if you took the money from a tax-deferred account where the tax efficiency of an annuity is irrelevant. All he or she seems to care about is the commission.

So now what you've actually got working for you is an $87,000 investment, not $100,000. There are all manner of surrender charges. It's not liquid.

Frankly, I've never seen an annuity that works as well as a nicely balanced portfolio of stocks and bonds. That's why I would shy away from annuities, unless they are a last resort for a person not wealthy enough to bear the risks of the capital markets. Indeed, annuities serve a useful purpose for individuals unable to bear the risks of the stock and bond markets, but, for wealthy individuals, I advise against annuities.

Here's what Larry Swedroe and Jared Kizer say about variable annuities in their book, *The Only Guide to Alternative Investments You'll Ever Need: The Good, the Flawed, the Bad, and the Ugly*:

> Some investment products are so complex in design that it is very difficult, if not impossible, for the average investor to fully understand the risks

entailed and the costs incurred. Make no mistake about it, the complexity is intentional. After all, if the investor fully understood the product, it is likely that he or she would never purchase it. That is why many of such products are truly "tourist traps"—designed to be sold, but never bought.

Education—or a good fee-only adviser who is not influenced by commission-based compensation—can be the armor that protects investors.

The overwhelming evidence from academic studies on variable annuities is clear: In general, these investments fall into the category of products that are meant to be sold, not bought.

Buyer beware!

GETTING THE BEST DEAL

I must be frank when it comes to getting the best deal for my clients. I risk making life insurance agents hate me, because I ask them if they'd like to bid on providing coverage. I'll say something like, "We've decided that my client needs five million dollars' worth of insurance. We like the idea of whole life [or whatever it is we've decided], and we'd like you to bid on that."

Life insurance agents typically don't respond very well to words like these because they have been taught to always be in control of the discussion.

It has been suggested that the greatest sales training in the world is that which is provided to life insurance agents. Their best trick is that after they have made the big pitch, they push the policy contract in front of you, slide the pen toward you, ask you to sign, and sit silently and motionless waiting for you to affix your signature under the pressure of the moment.

SIMPLICITY, SIMPLICITY, SIMPLICITY

When it comes to life insurance, my view is that the simpler the better.

I don't like universal life. I don't like variable life. I don't like universal/variable life. I do like ordinary term and ordinary whole life when there is a purpose for the coverage.

I recommend buying as much insurance as you can afford when you are as young as possible. That's when the premiums are the smallest. On the other hand, you should know that at age sixty, if you are in good health, you can probably buy whole life policy, fully paid up with no future premiums due, by writing a check for half the face value amount. So, if you are buying a $100,000 policy, you would write a single $50,000 check for it. It would pay off whenever you die.

Then again, suppose you don't want to pay cash for your life insurance and you want to put a de facto "mortgage" on it by paying a series of premiums.

When you pay this way, you're putting a mortgage on your life insurance policy. It's similar to how you can buy a car and pay cash. You can buy a home and pay cash. You can also buy life insurance and pay cash. Of course you can also buy all of these things (house, car, life insurance) over time if you're willing to pay the interest for financing the front-end cost.

When you start making regular premium payments, you're paying that original corpus, but you're financing it. You're engaging in *premium financing.* A lot of people don't realize this going in.

I have calculated the cost, and in today's market the interest rate for premium financing seems to be about 7.5%. So, if I can borrow money at less than that rate, say 1%, 2%, 3% or 4%, I'm better off borrowing at that more favorable rate and paying cash for my policy.

Ask your life insurance agent to explain the above to you. It's a complexity that is often not explained. Closing a life insurance sale is iffy enough for most agents without muddying up the water with one more detail.

MODIFIED ENDOWMENT CONTRACTS (MECs) AND CLOSING THE TAX LOOPHOLE

With life insurance, as in all financial matters, you have to be careful.

Prior to 1988, you could pay a single premium into a life insurance policy and have the cash value grow tax-deferred. At your death, the proceeds would flow tax-free to your beneficiaries. If you needed to borrow against the cash value of the policy in the meantime, the money would flow to you tax-free as a loan or withdrawal.

In 1988, Congress, in a thinly veiled effort to redistribute wealth, put an end to this loophole. It changed the law to say that life insurance policies that were over-funded too rapidly (as with a single large premium payment) would henceforth be classified as modified endowment contracts (MECs). The law eliminated the use of such policies as short-term savings vehicles by imposing stiff penalties and taxes on cash loans or withdrawals, i.e., tax-free access to cash values.

My personal strategy when buying whole life is to buy seven-pay life. I pay my premium every month, or once per year, for seven years. This means I don't violate the rules, the policy does not become an MEC, and I'm only suffering the onerous financing charge for the shortest amount of time possible.

I buy more life insurance every year. Every year I determine how much I can afford to spend and buy an additional policy on me and an additional policy on my wife. I actually would like to be the guy who dies with too much life insurance.

WHO SHOULD OWN THE POLICY?

In the 1950s, when everyone smoked and the men all wore snap-brim hats, life insurance was sold to men to protect the wife and children should something happen.

What a difference more than half a century makes. In an era of two-income households, where a family depends on the incomes of both spouse, it is often prudent for both the husband and the wife to have a policy.

Under most circumstances, life insurance proceeds are not subject to income tax, but they may be subject to federal and state estate taxes. If you own the policy on your own life and you die, the proceeds become part of your estate. That means they become subject to your "death tax." Rats. Not good.

A consultative life insurance advisor will be able to give you a variety of ideas about policy ownership including irrevocable life insurance trusts, bypass trusts, generation skipping trusts, your favorite charity, or a variety of other options beyond the scope of this chapter.

WHOLE LIFE?

When it comes to insurance, I personally like whole life for a number of reasons. First it provides "over the top" money for the surviving spouse. If something happens to you, there will be emotional grief and heartache, but there will also be practical challenges like bills to pay. Having a surplus of cash readily available enables the surviving beneficiaries to pay the bills so that he, she, or they can get on with their lives.

When someone dies, expenses are involved. If the estate is tied up in illiquid assets like real estate, satisfying those expenses can be a huge challenge. Cash from a life insurance policy can often fill that gap.

Life insurance can also pay off any straggling liabilities or any bank debts and provide currency to live on until the survivor(s) gets things sorted out. That's why I recommend that both spouses have insurance, and I like it to be fully paid-up whole life. This type of policy—unlike term insurance—does not expire. It remains in force forever and will pay off whenever the death of the insured occurs.

Regarding the conventional wisdom of "buy term and invest the rest," that sounds great, but I've never observed anybody with the discipline to execute this strategy.

In addition, whole life does have cash value. In most states, like your IRA, that cash is exempt from judgment.

There is also the fact that the right policy can help out if you are diagnosed with a terminal illness. Let's say you go in for your physical, and the doctor says,

"I hate to tell you this, but you've got six months to live. I know you feel great today, but you're going to go downhill fast." Well, you can take that medical statement to your life insurance provider and they will, in many cases, advance 50% of the death benefit of your life insurance policy. You can then use these funds to cover medical expenses. You would have ready cash to pay for someone to come into your house and take care of you as you're declining.

Based on the above, I view whole life as a sister product and an attractive alternative to long-term care insurance (LTCI). In fact, I don't recommend LTCI for the majority of my clients. If you don't have any money, LTCI might make some sense, but for people who are wealthy, I prefer self-insuring. In my view, in most situations, if your net worth is in excess of $3.5 million in today's dollars, you don't need to spend your money on LTCI.

My ultimate criticism with LTCI is it's absolutely "use it or lose it." In life insurance, you're going to use it because you're going to die, whereas the statistics on the utilization of LTCI speak against buying it. The vast majority of people, mercifully, never go into a nursing home. Once in a nursing home, the vast majority live less than eighteen months after admission. Of course, if you are very young and go into a nursing home, the LTCI might be beneficial, but be aware that LTCI rarely provides an infinite benefit and the likelihood of exhausting the finite benefit is high in this example.

I'll bet that someone has tried or will try to sell you long-term care insurance. I believe that people of means who like the idea of buying insurance would be better off with whole life insurance. It's "over the top" money for the surviving spouse, it's exempt from judgment, it has cash value should you burn through your other assets, there's the accelerated death benefit in the event of terminal illness, it increases the value of your estate for your beneficiaries, and it will not be, if planned well, taxable to those beneficiaries.

Just remember, if you start writing checks for LTCI and you write them forever, the odds are low that you'll use it at all. If you do use it, you probably won't use all of it. You'll die before you've used more care than you've paid for over the years. I prefer to take the money I could be spending on LTCI and adding it to my portfolio of stocks, bonds, and life insurance and self-insure for my contingent long-term care needs.

SELF-INSURING

I like to self-insure in some purposeful amount with all my insurance. I recommend to my clients that they self-insure to any extent that is purposeful.

Insurance premiums get lower when you implement a high deductible on your homeowners insurance and cars. If you're wealthy enough, you might consider liability only on your cars.

Self-insuring makes for lower premiums, which increases your disposable income, freeing up cash that can be spent or invested in earning assets like stocks, bonds, life insurance, and private deals.

Insurance is simply paying another party to bear a portion of your risk or risks. What risks can you bear? What risks can you not bear? Figure this out and purchase only insurance that protects your wealth efficiently and purposefully.

In closing, I view my risk management advisor—a professional whom I do not view as an insurance salesman—as one of the most important advisors to my clients and to me. Creating wealth is one challenge; maintaining wealth is another discipline. An excellent insurance advisor is an irreplaceable member of a team dedicated to protecting your wealth.

CHAPTER 8

SHARING YOUR WEALTH

In my experience as a wealth manager, I've observed that sometimes people are fortunate enough to have accumulated incremental unnecessary wealth, which is another way of saying "money they aren't going to need."

At some point, they may go through an inventory of their goals, values, needs, resources, and obligations, and a light bulb goes off in their minds. "I've got enough! I'm not going to outlive my money."

When, or if, a person might realize this state of sufficiency is a moving target. Teenagers are all ten feet tall and bulletproof. As we get older, we get more nervous. We become aware of the randomness of events and how unsettling incidents sometimes come over the horizon out of nowhere. Life is not always as safe and secure as it appears.

It is possible to reach the point where you know you've got enough. Often, when a person knows they don't need to worry about their own wealth, they then turn their attention to their heirs. Wanting their kids to own their home debt free or wanting to make sure their kids inherit the assets they have accumulated are common "wants" at this stage of development.

Considerations of life insurance for estate planning are common with the sole purpose of the contemplated life insurance being to pay an anticipated estate tax liability. This is a decision and an expenditure clients might not have made until they knew they had sufficient wealth.

As part of their estate planning, people may direct certain resources to their children, of course. But then, sometimes, a second light bulb will go off. "I've given my children enough. I don't want to create 'inheritance trainees.' I've done enough for my children and my heirs. So now I want to think about the world at large. What do I want to achieve with my money?"

The worthy causes in this world are legion. It might be the Boy Scouts of America because you were an Eagle Scout and feel Scouting did a lot for you. It could be your church, synagogue, mosque, or other place of worship. It might be the American Cancer Society because your mother died of cancer or the Alzheimer's Association because your father had dementia. Whatever you decide, it will be a uniquely personal decision.

BEATING THE MIDAS CURSE

Is it possible to leave too much money to your kids? I think it is, and so, too, do Warren Buffet and Bill Gates, according to their public statements.

My own feeling is that if you give too much money to your children, you deprive them of the joy and satisfaction of achieving on their own.

That's why I recommend reading *Beating the Midas Curse*.

With a foreword by my friend Connie Seay and written by Perry L. Cochell and Rodney C. Zeeb, two estate planning attorneys with years of experience in helping wealthy families plan their estates, *Beating the Midas Curse* examines the role of "affluenza," a destructive relationship with wealth, as a root cause of traditional planning collapse.

The publisher's description on Amazon.com continues:

[The book] also provides detailed analysis of the power of what has come to be known as the Heritage Process as a tool for keeping families, and their prosperity, intact for years. Plus, it describes the role of philanthropy as a major tool for combating the trans-generational effects of affluenza. Studies show that six out of ten affluent families will lose the family fortune by the end of the second generation. By the end of the third generation, nine out of ten of all affluent families have blown through the family wealth, and many have suffered terrible family strife.

In the Heritage Process, families learn through a guided discovery process how to make the values that have sustained and guided them to success the bedrock for their financial and estate planning. This "family before fortune" perspective is a powerful antidote to the grim statistics of family wealth collapse and family disunity.

Beating the Midas Curse was written for the families and individuals who will benefit most from values-based planning and for nonprofit organizations who want to help inform their constituents about the power of philanthropy in keeping families healthy and strong.

A FAMILY MISSION STATEMENT

We'll get into some of the mechanisms for charitable giving in a moment. Before we do, I'd like to say a word or two about inculcating a tradition of charitable giving within the family.

In my opinion, it is important for the matriarch and/or patriarch to sit their children down, when their children are old enough and responsible enough, and explain their plans for the disposition of their wealth upon their death. This has the potential to be a terrific dialogue and takes parenting to the next level—parenting your adult children!

My parents were always parents first and friends second. I aspire to be a good parent first and a friend to my kids second. If my children get mad at me and don't like me, I can live with that. But I will do my darnedest to be a good parent.

When your children are at the appropriate age, sit down with them and make them aware of the "who, what, when, where, and why" of your wealth—which is to say, the family's wealth—how the wealth was created, how the wealth has been maintained, the privileges of wealth, the responsibilities of wealth, and any commitments the wealth creators may have for charitable giving.

One tactic is to create a family mission statement. "What is our goal as a family when it comes to charitable giving?"

There are many firms that specialize in helping families develop such statements; the matriarch and the patriarch and all the children sit at the table with a third party. Sometimes children are more receptive to advice and guidance from independent third parties than they are from their parents. I know that some of the larger banks and trust companies provide the service of creating family mission statements, and there are many firms that specialize in this service.

You may consider it something of a gimmick, and you may be right. On the other hand, I have a friend who, with his family, has been meeting with someone once every year for over twenty years to create and update their family mission statement.

In addition to creating family mission statements, some of these firms will take the children away on a retreat where they will teach them about the responsibilities and the privileges of wealth and jump-start their life experience.

They might say, "It's nice that you're twenty-five years old and going to inherit $10 million, but let's talk about why that's happening. What responsibilities do you feel about that, and how will you live your life? Is it going to be the Rolex and the Maserati, or is it going to be achieving something and helping other people?"

DONOR-ADVISED FUNDS

This might come as a revelation if you have only recently contemplated charitable giving: You do not have to make "one-off" contributions to a specific charitable organization. You can instead set up a donor-advised fund that will periodically donate specified portions of your money to whomever you desire, provided that entity is a legitimate charity and meets, and continues to meet, conditions stipulated by you.

For example, suppose you want to give some of your money to a local park that you and your spouse have enjoyed for decades. Your first thought might be to give the money directly to the nonprofit organization that operates the park. You might direct that your money be used solely to maintain the lovely teak benches scattered throughout the park.

That's certainly doable. But who's to say for what purpose your money will actually be used? Who is going to enforce your directive, particularly after you're gone? Who knows if the park will even continue to be in existence?

This is why setting up a donor-advised fund, with the park as its beneficiary, is likely to be a much better way to go. When you fund such an entity, the money is removed from your estate and you get a tax deduction. But you still have control over how it is dispersed. Your money will be invested, and only the amounts you stipulate will go to the park—perhaps in perpetuity. After you die, there will be a trustee to make sure that your wishes are carried out.

You might, for example, set up a condition that says distributions from your donor-advised fund will continue to flow to the park as long as none of its land is sold for development. Should this condition be violated, you can stipulate that the earnings of your trust be directed to an entirely different charity.

Flexibility as to who the future beneficiary may or not be is essential. Further, naming the person, persons, or entity tasked with selecting future beneficiaries (the successor advisor) should your primary beneficiary cease to exist is a necessary element.

BUILDING A CRITICAL MASS OF MONEY

I issue many grants directly to organizations that my wife and I support. Additionally, we also have an auto-transaction setup that electronically sends a check monthly to our donor advised fund. This gives me great flexibility because I can dole out the money in the fund piecemeal or let it pile up and make a bigger donation somewhere down the road. I view our donor-advised fund as "budgeted giving."

We took the initiative to name successor advisors to the fund—our children, who will take over when we're gone. This gives our children a nice excuse to get together once a year and say, "Hey, Mom and Dad supported this cause and there's a bunch of money in this donor-advised fund, and it's our job to give it away. Where would we like to give that money this year?"

Donor-advised funds offer enormous flexibility. For example, I might insist that the money go to student competitive swimmers and to student musicians because both activities contributed substantially to my life. I might set things up so that my children could change the focus and vote on giving the money to some other cause.

The decision about who gets the money is uniquely personal, and the good news is you get to make it.

COMMUNITY FOUNDATION OPTIONS

Alternatively, I could stipulate that upon our ultimate demise the money in our donor-advised fund goes into our community foundations general fund as a fund in our names with disposition to be determined by the board of directors.

Regardless of your level of wealth, community foundations are a tool I recommend you explore.

They are inevitably nonprofits with boards who are dedicated to making sure that the money people contribute is distributed as the donors wish. These umbrella organizations and their boards and managers are your servants. You donate the money, they set up the fund, and they see to it that your money is used precisely as you wish: college scholarship money to graduates of a specific high school; support for the local humane society; grants to professionals working in the mental health field; or any other qualified nonprofit.

THE FAMILY FOUNDATION OPTION

Another and not mutually exclusive option is to create a family foundation.

Indeed, some people of wealth might say, "I've got this $20 million that I'm going to put into my family foundation. My children can then work for and derive income and benefits from the foundation." The kids now have employment in the form of managing the foundation and giving away money. Plus, they get to collect salary and benefits.

It may well be in your best interests to take that route. Just be aware that when you do so, under current tax law, you don't get as big a tax deduction as when you create and contribute to a donor-advised fund.

Also, the IRS has come down hard on some of these family foundations. The funds accumulate, and the next thing you know they've got a couple hundred million dollars piled up in there and the heirs are buying jets and condos and vacation homes.

If the expenses of running your family foundation exceed a certain percentage of the assets, the IRS is going to come down pretty hard because this looks to them to be an abuse of your foundation's status as a nonprofit.

With a family foundation, it would likely be imprudent to fly the kids first-class to Hawaii and have the foundation pay for the trip as they meet to decide how to distribute the money. This is the type of expense the IRS might be quick to criticize or disqualify.

CHARITABLE REMAINDER TRUST

Another option is setting up a charitable remainder trust.

In such a trust, as long as 10% goes to the designated beneficiary, you can receive an income stream from the money you've put in. That's fine, as long as you never dip below that 10%.

But you know what? You can also direct that the remainder 10% go to your family foundation or to your donor-advised fund.

Many people who are candidates for charitable giving have no idea what the possibilities are. Part of my job as a wealth manager is to make people aware of these things and connect them with the experts in these fields when giving becomes important to them.

I have one buddy who donates $500,000 to the Tulsa Community Foundation at the end of each year. He immediately sends them a spreadsheet detailing how much should be sent to a given organization and when for the coming year. He's systematic and purposeful in his giving in advance. He wants his money in something that is stable—cash or investment-grade bonds.

It is also possible to transfer other assets to donor-advised funds. I have a buddy with an expensive house in a small town, and he's not going to get much for it. I've suggested that he transfer title to his donor-advised fund. He can get a huge write-off for the reasonably appraised value of the home. On the other hand, if he tries to sell it, he might get significantly less. In this example, he gets a significant deduction, and the real cost to him is only the amount he would have received had he sold the home.

YOU NEED A PROFESSIONAL

If you're a tad confused, don't worry. This is a lot of data. I am attempting to present a thumbnail summary of a number of ways you can advantageously organize your charitable giving.

I hope to raise your awareness of this single fact: If you are a person of wealth and you want to make charitable contributions, you might benefit from professional guidance. There are tax, estate, and family implications, and they change every year with the whims of Congress.

Our firm does not provide that kind of hands-on guidance, but we do match our clients with charitable-giving specialists who can. If you are interested in pursuing one of these strategies, find a well-connected wealth manager in your own area and consult.

Setting up a donor-advised fund, a charitable remainder trust, a family foundation, or any of the other vehicles that benefit the world at large may just be a way for you to achieve financial immortality. Your money may live forever, constantly doing good in your name, long after you've left this earth. It is an admirable achievement.

So, if your "I have enough" light bulb is illuminated and you've provided for your children in the way you'd like, you might want to take a look at the many charitable options available. I recommend you seek professional help in ferreting out the best option.

CHAPTER 9

THE VALUE OF CONSULTATIVE WEALTH MANAGEMENT AND HOW TO FIND THE RIGHT ADVISOR FOR YOU

If you've read this far, there's a good chance that you're more than a little interested in what a wealth management advisor can do for you. But why do you need a wealth management advisor?

I could be flip and say, "Let me count the reasons."

Or, I could point out that although you made your millions manufacturing widgets and you know everything about widgets, you haven't spent your career as an investment professional and so you aren't, possibly, the most qualified to manage your investments.

Or, I could point out that the wealthiest people in the world utilize advisors. Successful folks know that they don't know everything, so they seek advice from the most elite specialists they can find.

These are not unpersuasive arguments. But they're not the real reasons wealthy people need wealth managers. To my mind, there are at least four things a wealth manager brings to the table, in addition to financial expertise:

1. Alignment of interests
2. Ability to help you identify your purpose
3. Objectivity
4. Investment discipline

ALIGNMENT OF INTERESTS

It often comes as a surprise to new home buyers that the real estate agent they contact for help does not work for them. He or she works for the seller of the property. (Unless, of course, they hire a buyer's agent.) Similarly, a commission-based stockbroker's loyalty is, by definition, to the firm employing him or her, not to his or her investor client.

Years ago, I was interviewed by a nationally prominent firm (NPF), before being recruited by a globally prominent firm (GPF). I asked this fellow at the NPF what he'd recommend in large-cap mutual funds. He pulled out a file drawer containing hundreds of folders, winked at me, and said that "I could use any of these but I like to use this one"—he held up a brochure—"because I get a bigger commission."

You go to Brokerage House A, and they're motivated to put you into Brokerage House A's funds. You go to Brokerage House B and they're motivated to put you into Brokerage House B's funds. Now, ask yourself: Do you think that House A has the best fund in every category? Or that House B does?

No. The "advisors" are told by their supervisors, "You will sell our cookin'. We've got a little restaurant and we manufacture investment products. This is what's on the menu, and this is what you serve."

A stockbroker's job is to generate as many dollars in trading commissions and fees for the firm that employs the stockbroker as possible. Their job is to get you to buy and sell stuff. They don't care whether you make money or not, since the commissions flow to them in either case. If they don't do it, they'll get fired, and the company will get somebody else who will do it.

Yet so many people rely on their stockbrokers as their personal investment advisors. Talk about inviting the fox into the henhouse!

Registered investment advisors (RIAs), in contrast, are not commission-based, they are fee-based. RIAs have a fiduciary responsibility to their clients to give them only the advice that's good for them. RIAs are prohibited from selling anything to make commissions. In fact, many RIAs don't sell anything that's commissioned.

The real difference between stockbrokers and independent registered investment advisors is the alignment of interests issue.

As an independent, fee-based advisor, the interests of my client and myself are aligned. We are on the same side of the table. The only way I'll make more money is if your wealth grows. Stockbrokers, in contrast, may or may not care if you make money or not. They are highly motivated to encourage you to buy the products their firm manufactures and encourage you to trade.

Therefore, I believe investors' interests are best served by fee-only registered investment advisors.

IDENTIFYING YOUR PURPOSE

When you're looking for an advisor, you want to find someone who has huge ears.

You're looking for an interested interviewer who asks you all kinds of questions to accurately understand your goals, values, needs, resources, and obligations.

Many portfolio managers and investment advisors ask perhaps a dozen pre-packaged questions (What is your income? When do you want to retire? What investments do you have?). They turn the crank on their computer models, and spit out a "plan."

For the vast majority of people, this works just fine. They don't have the flexibility that wealth brings. As a consequence, they have fewer possibilities. But if you have more than $1 million in investable assets, the picture changes dramatically.

Most of us are thoroughly conditioned to focus on increasing the value of our assets. (As Wordsworth said in 1807, "Getting and spending, we lay waste our powers.")

Wealth management is not about wealth creation. It's about maximizing the probability that you won't outlive your money and that you will achieve the goals you envision for your beneficiaries.

The majority of the wealthy folks I know created their wealth by taking calculated risks while utilizing their intellectual capital, time, and energy. Wealth can be created by stocks and bonds, but it's only likely if you have a long time. In my view, stocks and bonds are owned to provide for current and future currency.

Certainly, for most people, access to current and future currency are goals #1 and #2. A wealth management advisor can help you achieve these goals. But after that, what? A wealth management advisor, as I've shown, can help you identify and facilitate the other things you may want to do with your money.

For a person to be a good advisor, they have to be able to determine what your purpose is. Until they know your purpose, how can they give you any useful advice?

WHAT CAN I SELL YOU TODAY?

A bad advisor would come in with a sales pitch and say, "Well, it's sure nice to see you today. You know, I got some news from our consultants in New York City, and we think that the head of Microsoft just sold fifty million shares. He says it's because he is diversifying his wealth, but I think that he really knows more than we do, so we have a 'sell' rating on Microsoft."

They come in and start pitching you on a bunch of random ideas. They often refer to their pitch as "their best idea right now."

If you start swinging at these pitches, your portfolio will end up looking like so much shiny confetti that spews from a piñata. Have any of these deal pitchers ever asked you how much cash you need to feel good, how much is a purposeful amount for a currency reserve, how much to put in your long-term portfolio, and how much risk is appropriate for that?

The right advisor is going to want to know as much as possible about what drives your life before they offer any advice at all. The wrong advisor is going to say, "Our crystal ball is better than anybody else's. You should let us gamble with your money."

Let me give you an example of the kind of analysis you aren't likely to hear from a stockbroker or your mutual fund company's advisory service.

A client will come into my office worried about whether he has enough. (This usually happens when the stock market takes a dip.) My goal is to help my clients run their personal affairs like a business. At this point, I will start cash-flow forecasting. I will ask:

How much is in your checking account right now? How much do you plan to spend between now and the end of the year? How much income will you have by year end from a variety of sources, and how dependable are they?

All right, so now you've got X in cash, money is coming in, money is going out, and at the end of the year you're going to have Y. Now let's go to next year. We're going to start the year with Y, so what are your income and expenses going to be next year?

Sometimes, we'll take this exercise out for five or ten years.

Then we'll go over to the asset side and evaluate whether or not the client has a high likelihood of remaining wealthy to 100.

By doing this exercise, we can accurately determine whether our client is accumulating wealth, whether there is a need to annuitize from existing net worth, and whether or not the recent market dip is worth worrying about.

In almost every instance the above scenario plays out with our clients making statements like, "Gosh, I'm really in good shape," or "I guess I don't need to worry about the market dip." This is our goal—helping our clients understand they are wealthy and they are freed from financial worries.

ACCESS TO CASH IS THE KEY

As an advisor, I believe my first job is to make sure that my client has a purposeful amount of cash on hand in a checking or savings account for emotional purposes—it's whatever amount the client needs to sleep well at night.

Then we're going to set aside a "currency reserve" of short-term investment-grade bonds. The amount in this currency reserve will be purposeful and reflect all of the known needs and contingencies facing our client.

I disagree with the Suze Orman advice that you should have ninety days of cash on hand. Suze is smart, but her advice paints with too broad of a brush. Ninety days of cash may be fine for a recent college graduate, but it isn't uniquely personal and probably isn't enough for an eighty-year-old worrywart.

Actually, I believe that you don't need to have cash at all; you need to have *access* to cash. Of course, this is my view, and, although I will discuss it with my clients, I won't insist that they think like I think.

I would like to see my clients holding less cash and more short-term investment-grade bonds. I call these kinds of bonds "enhanced cash," because the money is readily accessible yet it earns a better rate of interest than money market funds and has a high probability of out-performing inflation.

At retirement I believe you should have ten to twenty years' worth of your lifestyle burn rate in the combination of your checking account and currency reserve. You might say, "Okay, my lifestyle burn rate is $10,000 a month. Since I'm going to get $4,000 from Social Security, my shortfall is $6,000 a month, which is $72,000 year. That's $720,000 a decade or $1,440,000 for two decades."

Suppose we decide to set aside twenty years' worth of lifestyle burn rate. We might put $1,440,000 into short-term, investment grade bonds and put whatever is not in the checking account and currency reserve into a long-term portfolio (which may also have some bonds in it).

Let's assume the amount in your currency reserve returns 2%. That's $28,000 a year. You need $72,000, so with your $28,000 in earnings, you're only going to withdraw $44,000 each year. Your money is going to last way longer than twenty years!

What happens when this client, who wants to know he has enough, comes in to see us because negative noise is emanating from the financial media and the market is down? I can demonstrate that he has access to currency for more than twenty years and the long-term portfolio on top of that.

This scenario is about as rock solid as it can get.

The long-term portfolio investments have exposure to the market, of course. But those funds may never be needed. If they are needed, it won't be for twenty, twenty-five, or thirty years. So the inter-period ups and downs of the stock market don't impact the client's access to currency for decades, assuming that future spending approximates projected spending.

This is when my clients will typically lean back in their chairs and say, "This is so helpful. I had never thought about it like this. I'm okay, aren't I?"

Yes, you are. You may have other things to worry about, but one thing won't be how you're going to pay your bills—not for a long, long time.

OBJECTIVITY

We've already spoken about how impossible it is for an advisor to be objective when a sales commission is involved. But that's not what I'm referring to here.

When it is your money, your goals, and your lifestyle seemingly at risk, it can be difficult to remain emotionally unattached. It might be shares of stock your father gave you on your fiftieth birthday that you're reluctant to sell, even though it is the worst performing stock you own. (We call this an "heirloom" investment.) It could be a lakeside second home that no one visits anymore. It might be your ownership stake in a money-losing business.

Serving as your personal CFO, a wealth management advisor can "do the math" for you. He or she may be able to broach topics (like selling the lake house) that even your spouse might be afraid to mention.

A good advisor can also identify options for your consideration that perhaps you were not aware existed. This is intuitive given the "two heads are better than one" truism. It's a combination of being able to see additional opportunities and then helping you think through them objectively.

INVESTMENT DISCIPLINE

Is your portfolio up? Is it down? Take a lesson from Marty Schottenheimer, the head coach of several NFL teams. Marty was my next door neighbor in Kansas City. Marty had what he called "the twenty-four-hour rule." If his football team played somebody on Sunday and they won big, they were permitted to celebrate all they wanted for twenty-four hours. "We can high-five, and we can feel good, but now the twenty-four hours are over, and we need to be planning for the future and doing everything we can to control what we can control."

Likewise, if they lost in a very disappointing game on Sunday, everybody would be depressed. "Well, you're allowed to be depressed for twenty-four hours. But after twenty-four hours, let's remember what our big goals are and let's get on with achieving them and not get all bogged down."

It is natural to feel elated when you get that quarterly statement showing that your holdings shot up; it's natural to feel depressed when your holdings go down.

Remember that what we're talking about is "transient valuations." You still own the same stocks, bonds, and mutual funds each month. It just so happens that they are valued differently on a day-to-day basis. The same logic applies whether they are valued up or valued down. There is no reason to feel depressed should the next statement show that your holdings are worth less or elated if the next statement shows they are valued higher.

If you have a sound plan, there is certainly no reason to change your plan as a result of transient valuations. We believe that part and parcel of a good plan is periodically rebalancing a portfolio. Rebalancing is, essentially, mechanical market-timing enabling investors to benefit by the transient momentum our markets demonstrate. Rebalancing, effectively, sells assets that have out-performed under the assumption that they advanced too far too fast and are positioned for reversion to the mean. Likewise, rebalancing purchases assets that have under-performed given the assumption that they have declined too far too fast and are positioned for their own reversion to the mean.

Rebalancing is an example of the kind of discipline that an advisor brings to the table. If the value of your portfolio has dropped, let's sit back and take a look at your plan. Do you still have your target cash? Yes. Is the value of your purposeful currency reserve still intact? Yes. Has your long-term portfolio of stocks and bonds vacillated? It may have vacillated up or down, but it doesn't matter because we expected vacillation and you're living out of your cash and currency reserve.

Do you see how different this is from looking for the next shiny investment in pursuit of incremental unnecessary wealth?

A good advisor will advise you to become emotionally indifferent to good or bad news contained in account valuation statements that arrive in your mailbox. If you've got a good plan, you know you've got a good plan. Quarterly statements supply interesting information, but it isn't particularly useful information and it should neither tweak your emotions nor move you to action.

Another side of investment discipline is keeping a client on course. I spend a tremendous amount of time reminding my clients what their purpose is.

It's not unusual for clients to come in and say they are considering investing in a restaurant with their son-in-law or they want to drill an oil well in their backyard. There's an old saying that what drives the stock market is fear and greed. My feeling is that an advisor is there to anesthetize fear and greed. No decision should ever be made because of fear or greed, and a good advisor will persuasively remind you of that.

Let's make our decisions on what we know and what's practical and whether or not those decisions implement our purposeful plan.

WHEN TO HOLD AND WHEN TO FOLD

I don't think of myself as having a "bedside manner," but I suppose it's necessary sometimes.

Recently I had a conversation with an older woman who had invested in several private deals that were supposed to pay off, but didn't. "Everybody's telling me what to do," she says. "But I've been cheated before. These days I don't know who to trust."

It soon became clear to me exactly what this woman should do with her money. She was so emotionally involved and had such a history of bad deals that she would not be comfortable with any investment advice unless it included the word "guaranteed."

My first suggestion had been very, very conservative: short-term investment grade bonds. But that wasn't guaranteed enough for her. I knew that the bonds were her best risk/reward course, but because of her past history, she couldn't emotionally tolerate even that minimal amount of risk.

The fact is that not only do you need to have a good plan; the plan needs to feel good to you. My recommendation of bonds did not feel good to her.

So I said, "Here's what you ought to do. Just go down to three or four different banks (so you are completely covered by FDIC insurance) and buy a bunch of CDs. Buy three-year CDs because the returns are higher. If all of a sudden you decide you need the money, you can always go and cash in the CDs. [At that time, all you paid for cashing in a CD was ninety days' interest forfeiture.] Even if you hold the CD for only two years, net of interest forfeiture you'll still earn more than you would in a money market."

When working with a client, it is important to be as objective as possible. But sometimes you have to go with the emotional flow. A plan that doesn't feel good to a client *ipso facto* is not good for the client.

FINDING THE RIGHT ADVISOR

Finding the right advisor isn't an easy task. For one thing, there's the matter of proximity. Some people want to deal only with advisors who live out of town because they've only got $1 million and they want their neighbors to think they've got $100 million. Others have the $100 million and want neighbors to think they've only got $1 million.

The logic isn't exactly clear here since no one would want to deal with any advisor who didn't observe the strictest confidentiality. But that's how some people feel.

For others, it's important that their advisor live within ten miles, so they can go into the office for face-to-face meetings, see them at the Friday night ballgame, bump into him or her at restaurants, know who their friends are, know their associates, and be comfortable with them.

On the other hand, I have a number of clients who are hundreds of miles away. We typically communicate via Skype video calls. Skype-to-Skype calls are free, and with today's laptops with their built-in video cameras and microphones, the process is painless.

THE FAMILY-OFFICE EXPERIENCE

Regardless of geographical location, I'd say that the touchstone for identifying wealth management advisors who are likely to be right for you is this: Do they offer the "family office" experience, and if so, are they fee-based or commission-based?

No matter how much you may like them personally, you don't ever want to entrust your money to someone who is commission-based. That rules out stockbrokers and insurance salespeople masquerading as "estate planners."

Firms offering a fee-based family office experience
are, in contrast, "all in" for you. Such firms will have a
deep interest in all aspects of your financial life. These
firms' interests will be completely aligned with yours.

By the way, our firm, and any firm worth its salt,
will be happy to identify advisors who offer the family-
office experience in your geographical area once it
becomes evident that you want, need, and prefer face-
to-face advice. There are no guarantees, of course, but
a firm that aspires to be genuinely helpful will use
their network in the field to assist you in finding a
suitable wealth management advisor in your market
area.

Working with a wealth management advisor
requires a leap of faith. You need to do the best you can
on due diligence.

On one point you must be absolutely inflexible.
Whichever advisor you select, it is imperative that
they use an independent, third-party custodian for
your assets.

Ever wonder how the Bernie Madoff-type Ponzi
schemes thrived for so many years? The Ponzi scheme
firms did not have an independent third-party keeping
track of client assets and sending those clients a statement every month saying, "Here are your assets and
here is what they are currently worth." Oh, there were
statements from Madoff, but they were faked by the
criminals involved. No investor should ever give away

the third-party custodian piece. A third-party custodian is absolutely essential.

In my view a consultative wealth management advisor is a valuable resource. I strongly encourage anybody seeking to make work optional and maintain that status to engage one.

CHAPTER 10

TRANSITIONS: MODIFYING YOUR PLAN

Throughout this book, I have emphasized a comprehensive approach to wealth management, an approach that included clarifying your goals, making smart investment decisions, managing your taxes, planning your estate, protecting your wealth, and sharing your wealth while you're living and after you're gone.

I have emphasized developing a plan and sticking to that plan, regardless of the gyrations of the stock and bond markets. I have done this because I know the human tendency to flit from one thing to another when changing markets play on our instincts for fear and greed.

Stay the course. Stick to the plan. Come in at any time and let's review things. I know I don't need to remind you again about the benefits of a fee-based wealth management advisor. Fee-only advisors have no incentive whatsoever to encourage you to buy or sell stocks, bonds, or other securities. Your fee-based advisor is, essentially, on retainer for you, and you should demand the time of your advisor whenever and as much as you want.

Years ago, when a ship encountered heavy weather at sea, the captain would deploy a cone of canvas called a "sea anchor" off the stern. Submerging and filling with water, the sea anchor would keep the ship pointed into the wind, meaning the vessel would not veer off to port or starboard—to possibly founder on the shoals. That's what a thoroughly crafted financial plan does for you during financial storms.

But things in your life do change.

The goals, values, needs, resources, and obligations your plan is built to serve may change. A brief inventory of possibilities includes: death of a spouse; loss of your job; getting a new job; winning the lottery; selling your business; the death of a parent; inheritance; divorce; new marriage; more children; loss of a child.

Or the ultimate game changer—you retire.

Retirement is actually the biggest change most people face, and, of course, it affects planning. In the simplest sense, retiring moves a person (or couple), in many cases, from wealth accumulating to wealth annuitization.

In the best of all possible worlds, people would begin creating and executing a plan as soon as they enter the labor force. But we all know that rarely happens. More than likely, the investor turns fifty-ish and begins to realize that retirement is coming.

So they come in, and we develop a plan. For the next fifteen years, we work that plan with only minor modifications. Then Social Security becomes a factor. Retirement becomes a factor. Parents die, and they inherit. God forbid, but health problems may develop. Goals and what they want to accomplish with their lives may change.

So the plan must change with their changed needs.

A good wealth manager will not only make this happen, he or she will foresee such needed changes and plan for them.

TRANSITIONS

Often our focus is on retirees. Over the years, I've conducted dozens of interviews with people I consider to be centers of influence—owners and operators of retirement communities and living centers, providers of geriatric care and management services, and, of course, retirees themselves.

One of the things I have come to realize as a result of these interviews is that the word "transition" is a very important word to get one's head around, especially when serving the retirement community. That's because retirees tend to go through a fairly accelerated number of transitions once they leave the workplace.

While you're working, things tend to look pretty much the same from day to day. When retirement and the aging process come along, things start changing fast. They change on multiple fronts. In my experience, consultative wealth management of the sort we practice can be invaluable on each of these fronts.

One front, of course, is income. Most retirees will be transitioning from a paycheck to something else. Their chief concern at that point is, "Will I have enough? How do I make sure I don't run out?"

Of course, health may also become an issue. When health is involved, people want to know what kind of help is available if it is needed. You might not think of turning to your wealth manager for guidance on something like this. But that's exactly the kind of family-office service we believe you should seek. In fact, we often talk with nice folks about introducing them to a geriatric manager to help their parents with mowing their lawn and doing and handling other chores. We have also introduced clients to life coaches and specialist physicians.

Another transition is transition of lifestyle. Here's where I don't like the word "retirement" because it implies that you're done. Your daily schedule and lifestyle may change, but during retirement there's still a lot left to do.

What do you still want to accomplish? What are the possibilities? We help clients with that. Sometimes it can be very difficult for people to manage this transition.

Their jobs were part of their identity and the source of their self-esteem. Now the job is gone from their lives.

Another possible transition is residence. People ask, "Where is the best place for me to age?" and "How do I make my home more senior-friendly?"

Advisors can help here as well. Among other things, we'll help clients realize that their neighborhoods will change as people die or move elsewhere. You can have the most senior-friendly house in the world, but if living there means you'll be emotionally and relationally isolated, it might be better to live in a retirement community or senior living center where you'll have plenty of neighbors.

There's another strand that often gets overlooked, and it is the one I call family transition. "How is my relationship with my family going to change as I age? I have been the caregiver; will I now be the object of caregiving from other family members?" There are all kinds of ramifications.

If any one of these various transitions isn't considered and well planned for they can create stress and lead to all manner of avoidable problems.

This makes perfect sense when you think about it. We have all this information about our clients, and we focus on pulling all the threads together. Then we have regular meetings with our clients to see if anything has changed in their lives or if they are facing issues now that they weren't facing the last time we talked or met.

For a comprehensive advisor, working with clients is an ongoing process. It's the right model, I believe, to guide someone through the various transitions that a retiree is going to experience.

WHEN TO START

So, when should you get started? Well, twenty- and thirty-year-olds typically don't want to hear about retirement. On the other hand, some folks are ready for this message earlier than others. We have clients in their twenties who are very thoughtful and conservative. They are focused on creating wealth, sharing wealth, and being able to achieve and maintain "work is optional" status. I'm always impressed and inspired by these youngsters.

Fifty-five or so is actually the age that most people begin to think about retirement. They recognize that retirement and aging are coming. That's often the sweet spot of where to begin a relationship. The person is typically receptive, so we can say, "Here are some things to consider. Let's plan now."

I want to emphasize, however, that I'm only speaking about retirement planning here. Certainly you should begin the other elements of your wealth management planning as soon as possible.

TRANSITIONING AWAY FROM
CONVENTIONAL WISDOM

I'd like to close with a word or two of common sense regarding wealth management that might help you to transition your thinking today.

Wall Street loves rules of thumb, but I think that painting with a broad brush is less than ideal.

For example, it is said that to determine what percentage of your portfolio should be in stocks, subtract your age from one hundred. The idea is that bonds are safer than stocks, and the older you get, the safer you want your investments to be.

But this notion is severely flawed. It fails to look at the whole picture. It doesn't look at life expectancy, age at retirement, how much money you have, your cost of living, your other resources, or your mailbox income. It is a brush that's too broad.

Another canard is the one that says, "You should always have three to six months' of salary in an emergency fund." I think that's ridiculous. It might be a great rule if you're twenty-three years old, but it' probably too low when you're sixty.

Or how about: "Set aside 10% of your gross income for savings. Always save 10%." That's a nice starting point, but what if you're sixty years old and you haven't saved anything? Saving 10% off the top probably isn't going to get you to "work is optional" status.

Or, "To retire comfortably, your investments must generate 70% to 80% of the income you received while working." That's ridiculous, too. It doesn't take into account things like your life expectancy or the extent of your wealth. It suggests investing for income in favor of investing for total return, which, I believe, is a huge mistake. Investing for total return is a far superior strategy—but only with some of your money.

How about: "The stock market will give you a 10% annual return." That's a very bad rule. It's actually based on the Ibbotson-Sinquefield study of long-term equity returns done in 1976. While it is true that the stock market has grown at about 10% annually from 1927 to the present day, there is no guarantee that the next eighty-five years will play out like the last eighty-five years. There may be many companies that are going to grow at more than 10% over the next thirty years, but when you say, "The stock market will grow at 10%," that's too broad. It doesn't specify large-cap or small-cap growth or domestic or foreign, and it makes an assumption that I would not bet my retirement on.

Then there is this: "Life insurance benefits should equal five times your current income." I think this is like De Beers proclaiming that the cost of an engagement ring should total three months' salary. It's a ploy to move more product. The problem is the focus on income rather than expenses. You can't be solving for income without thinking about expenses. Maybe having a policy that pays five times your current income is too much for some people and not nearly enough for others.

SUMMARY

The key message of this chapter has been to raise awareness of the transitions that occur in life.

The takeaways are three-fold:

First, begin your wealth management planning as early as possible—the younger the better. But when you enter your fifties, start thinking seriously about your retirement. That will almost certainly mean modifying your plan.

Second, a good wealth manager can do much more than help you design and execute a uniquely personal plan; he or she can also provide many ancillary services, expertise, and introductions at no additional charge. Indeed, you shouldn't have to ask; your wealth manager should already be asking you the questions that reveal the needs.

Third, a good plan today may not be a good plan tomorrow. A plan needs to be tested regularly for adequacy.

Transitions are part of life and your uniquely personal plan needs to transition in harmony with changes in your life.

CONCLUSION

As a high net worth individual, you will have investment options that most people do not have. Yet, you might not be immediately aware of the frivolity of many of the options. Unless you're a full-time professional investor, managing money is probably not the central focus of your life and it's almost impossible to separate the wheat from the chaff in the world of investment products.

Hopefully managing money isn't the central focus of your life—unless it has become your primary form of entertainment. The reason I began this book with "A Bowl Full of Life" was to emphasize the value of focusing on the vast array of important things life has to offer.

Wealth management is about bearing purposeful investment risks, optimizing your taxation, crafting your estate plan, minimizing random (and obvious) risks with insurance, and buttoning up your charitable intent.

Concept #1 is that the investment piece of wealth management should be about making smart financial decisions. That means using passively managed funds that charge the lowest fees and are the most tax efficient to create a purposeful asset allocation. Historical data and statistical analysis point to this conclusion. I believe any student of the capital markets will ultimately draw a similar conclusion.

Concept #2 can be summarized in two words: comprehensive consultation.

Excellent advisors will listen to you at length and bring their powers to bear on every aspect of your financial life. The mission will be to understand everything, identify gaps, suggest solutions, introduce you to experts, and make sure that your advanced planning needs—taxation, estate planning, insurance coverage, and charitable intent—are recognized and a thoughtful plan is in place.

Wealth management is not "create a plan, set it, and forget it." Wealth management is an ongoing process.

Developing your plan is the opening movement of an entire symphony. Successive movements in the symphony may emphasize different themes as your goals, values, needs, resources, and obligations change. An excellent advisor will anticipate these changes and be with you every step of the way.

We strongly recommend that you identify a firm that offers a family-office experience. A firm of this type will help you with all of the major topics covered herein—investments, taxes, estate planning, insurance needs, and charitable giving. The best wealth managers help clients with all of the above and much more.

Clients of wealth managers do not suffer the speculation and conjecture offered by financial advisors masquerading as wealth managers. Clients of true wealth managers receive comprehensive consultative wealth management. A firm delivering a family-office experience will be dedicated to your receiving the same.

I hope you will be able to make work optional and maintain that status. I hope you will be able to live well, enjoy a life free of financial concerns, and be able to fulfill your goals.

Assess your purpose and move forward!

Tom Warburton's
Purposeful Wealth Management

What if there were a way to think purposefully about the major wealth management decisions each of us must make?

Wouldn't it be great if someone could explain to us—in plain and simple English—the basics we must know to implement purposeful wealth management?

At last, here's good news.

Written for every person that wants to "make work optional and maintain that status," Purposeful Wealth Management reveals a process for ascertaining your uniquely personal goals, values, needs, resources, and obligations, then purposefully orchestrating the five key elements of wealth management—investments, taxation, estate planning, insurance, and charitable intent.

Purposeful Wealth Management is the one and only book you'll need to have a successful wealth management experience.

About the Author

Tom Warburton is the founder of Warburton Capital Management, a firm dedicated to helping its clients "make work optional and maintain that status."

Tom and his team of expert advisors assist successful business owners, corporate executives, and professionals to purposefully implement their wealth management intentions in a disciplined and systematic manner.

A frequently published and quoted wealth management advisor, Tom is a lifelong entrepreneur with a history of happy family life, civic contributions and athletic achievements.

Tom served in a variety of trust and private banking roles for the Citizens National Bank of Waukegan, the First National Bank of Chicago, the Bank of Oklahoma, and JPMorgan before founding Warburton Capital Management. He graduated from Indiana University with a BA in comparative religious studies.

CPSIA information can be obtained
at www.ICGtesting.com
Printed in the USA
FFOW02n2243260518
46869311-49112FF